Divorced & Scared No More!

Dating after Divorce—From Lemons to Zesty Lemon Sorbet

By Tasher

Poems by Tony Haynes

Contributions & Foreword by William Kenly

Dating after Divorce

Copyright © 2016 by T asher & Tony Haynes

Divorced and Scared No More!
Dating after Divorce—From Lemons to Zesty Lemon Sorbet
by Tasher & Tony Haynes

Printed in the United States of America
Cover Designer Jihyeon Joung
Book Design & Formatting Sandraspeed Formatting Expert

All rights reserved solely by the author. The author guarantees all contents are original and do not infringe upon the legal rights of any other person or work. No part of this book may be reproduced in any form without the permission of the author. The views expressed in this book are not necessarily those of the publisher.

To my children and grandchildren: Thank you for always being there for me. You are the best cheerleaders anyone could ever hope to have in their life. I love you to the moon and back to infinity now and forever. You are the loves of my life and my reason for being!

A special thanks to my brother Bob. You always believed and encouraged me to do my best. Plus, you never stopped reminding me what a wonderful world this is. Even when things seem so very dark, I always have him and God to lean on for support.

Thank you to everyone that allowed me to share your experiences in this book. ***As with the entire series, out of respect for everyone's privacy, some identifying information (including but not limited to names) has been changed. I write with a Christian point of view, but if you are not a Christian, please substitute the higher power within your life.***

This book is also dedicated to everyone who jumped back into the dating pool and shared so many moving, funny, and helpful stories of life and dating after divorce. Any stories told within any of my books that include names specific events et cetera have been changed to protect people's privacy. The site Divorced and Scared NO More was online from 2012 until 2019. You can still follow us on Facebook and Twitter.

Feel free to thumb through to the chapter that applies to your situation in the order you wish. As you are reading this book, think about who you are going to give it to after you have finished. If you have someone in mind, put their name or initials on a post-it, and stick it inside the back cover of the book. When you have completed and no longer need the book, give it to them. Pass it on with love and the intention of letting go.

You may wonder why my pen name is Tasher. When I was in high school, we would have to put our names at the top of the paper with only the first initial of your first name, followed by your last. When my classmate was handing out papers, he called me Tasher. From that moment on during high school, I had the nickname Tasher. When I started writing the books, I wanted to use a pen name, so I would not hurt anyone's feelings regarding anything I might put within. I thought and thought about different names one afternoon the boy that had given me that nickname so many years ago called. The first words out of Bill's mouth was "Hey Tasher," so decided God must be sending me a GodWink to use my old nickname as my pen name.

—Tasher

Dating after Divorce

Every ending is almost always a little sad, even when you are looking at a wonderful new beginning.

Contents

REINVENTING THE WILL IX

FOREWORD .... **X**

CHAPTER 1

LESSONS TO LEARN ABOUT YOURSELF **1**

    DO YOU LOVE MORE? 4
    IS IT POSSIBLE TO FIND LOVE AGAIN? 6
    THE DEEPER THE HOLE, THE HIGHER THE BUILDING 9

CHAPTER 2

PREPARE YOURSELF TO DATE **10**

    ARE YOU READY TO TAKE THE PLUNGE? 10
    WAYS TO FEEL DATEABLE WHILE HAPPILY DIVORCED 13
    WHERE TO FIND LOVE 15
    THE MOST COMMON DATING BLUNDERS TO AVOID 16
    DATING IS A TIME TO HAVE FUN AND MEET NEW PEOPLE 21
    NOT A SOCIAL BUTTERFLY? THAT'S OKAY! 22
    IS IT OKAY TO DATE MORE THAN ONE PERSON? 23
    EMOTIONAL ATTRACTION IS STRONGER THAN PHYSICAL 26

REMEMBER, IT'S NOT EASY BEING GREEN 26
SINGLE AGAIN AND DATING WITH CHILDREN 29
COLORED BY WHITE LIGHT 34

CHAPTER 3

BE A PERSPICACIOUS DATER 35

FOUR TYPES OF DATING STRATEGIES 35
    Someone Showed Me Attention 35
    Deal Breakers versus Checklists 39
    Serial Daters 43
    A Perspicacious Dater 45
WHY MEN (OR WOMEN) DON'T APPROACH YOU 47
RULES FOR DATING? 49
IF LIFE WASN'T SO HARD, WE'D VALUE IT LESS 52

CHAPTER 4

DATING SAFETY 53

DATE SMART AND SAFE, NOT FAST AND RECKLESS 53
DON'T TRUST IN OTHERS' BACKGROUND CHECKS 55
HAVING YOUR SMART PHONE WORK FOR YOU 57
BEWARE! YOUR DRINK MAY HAVE A DATE RAPE DRUG! 59
THE COURAGE TO CARE 64

CHAPTER 5

ONLINE DATING 65

DATING HAS CHANGED 65
SOCIAL NETWORKS AND ONLINE DATING 66
YOUR ONLINE DATING PROFILE IS AN ADVERTISEMENT ABOUT YOU 68
NETIQUETTE 75
SETTING UP AN EMAIL ACCOUNT TO USE WITH PEOPLE YOU MEET ONLINE 78
THE PROCESS FOR DATING ONLINE 80
WHAT ARE THE ODDS? SAFETY IS AN ISSUE FOR BOTH SEXES 88
PRISON TATTOOS 90
SAFETY TIPS FOR ONLINE DATING 92
A DATE MAY BE DIFFERENT FROM HOW THEY PRESENT THEMSELVES ONLINE .. 93
IS SOMEONE TRYING TO CATFISH ME OR IS THIS PERSON REAL? 95
ARE THEY HIDING SOMETHING? 102

MEANT TO BE 108

CHAPTER 6

PREPARING FOR YOUR DATE 109

  WHAT TO WEAR 109
  TO RING OR NOT TO RING? 111
  ADVICE TO KEEP IN MIND FOR YOUR MEET AND GREET OR THE FIRST DATE 112
  LET THE RESTAURANT HELP YOU 116
  A FEW DON'TS WHILE DATING 118
  TALK AND GET TO KNOW WHO YOU'RE DATING 120
  THE GREATNESS OF JUST BEING 122

CHAPTER 7

DATING CHALLENGES 123

  DUMP THE CHECKLIST, BUT DON'T SETTLE 123
  RUN FROM THE ALWAYS-RIGHT PERSON 125
  LEARN THE ART OF WALKING AWAY AND SAYING NO 127
  SINGLE AGAIN AND AGAIN AND 129
  DEALING WITH DATING BURN-OUT 131
  GETTING OUT OF DATING BURNOUT 134
  MAY FREEDOM FALL IN LOVE WITH YOU 137

CHAPTER 8

IMPORTANT POINTS TO REMEMBER WHEN DATING 138

  DON'T BRING YOUR EX ON YOUR DATE 138
  MISSING PHYSICAL ASPECTS OF A RELATIONSHIP 140
  IF A FRIEND SAYS, "DON'T DATE THEM," LISTEN 144
  MAKE DATING FUN 146
  I GOT MY FEET WET 148

CHAPTER 9

THE DOGS OF DATING 149

  THE FIRST DATE 152
  THE CABLE LADY 155
  MATCHMAKER.COM 158
  PARENTS WITHOUT PARTNERS 159

ALICIA 160
GIVERS, TAKERS, AND DATING 163
LIZ   167
MARY 168
CAROL 168
KATERINA 170
DATING AND WHY HIPAA IS A GOOD IDEA 171
EVEN LOVE SOMETIMES MUST SCRATCH ITS HEAD & WONDER 175

CHAPTER 10

DATING AFTER DIVORCE: STORIES AND A FEW LITTLE EXTRA ANECDOTES 176

THE CRAZY PSYCHIATRIST 176
PRIVATE SECURITY CONTRACTOR 180
DON'T SKIP DATING RULES 183
NOT ALL CROSS-DRESSERS ARE THE SAME 185
LAKE PARTY 188
TEXTING FREDDY AND EDDY 191
YOU'VE BEEN MARRIED HOW MANY TIMES? 192
ALWAYS ASK IF THERE IS SOMETHING ABOUT THEM YOU NEED TO KNOW 194
AM I TOO PICKY? 196
DARREL HAD AN INTERESTING PATH TO FINDING HIS LOVE 197
A QUICK STOP TO PICK UP SOME MONEY 198
PHIL MET FOXY ON A FREE ONLINE DATING SITE 200
BLIND DATES CAN BE A DREAM OR A NIGHTMARE 201
IN THE NEW MODERN BLENDED FAMILY: EVEN IF YOU HAD NOTHING TO DO WITH IT 203
THE HEART KNOWS 205
LITTLE BITTY BABIES 206

CHAPTER 11

PATIENCE, CAUTION, AND A SENSE OF HUMOR 207

CONNECTIVITY 209
ZESTY LEMON SORBET 210
THROUGH THE TOUGHEST TIMES 211
I AM MY OWN HERO 212

CONTACT AND LINKS 218

** DEAR READER --FINAL THOUGHTS * 219

Dating after Divorce

Reinventing the Will

*S*o often we must make ends meet

*A*nd take the bitter with the sweet.

*M*otivation is hard to come by;

*P*reservation insists that some die.

*L*ike vinyl & eight track tape,

*E*volution brings a changing shape.

*L*ove loves on unchanged and still

*I*t reinvents the will.

*F*or when the will is reinvented

*E*ach dream can then be implemented …

… *And seen the way God sent it*

—***Tony Haynes***

Foreword

If my grandmother had visited me from Heaven during the time of my divorce and told me about all the different nooks and crannies of my life that were about to change, and if she were to methodically and lovingly explain the new challenges that would arise and possible choices for each, and if my she were to gently offer me a few basic guidelines and touchstones that might help with each of my new life's decisions—if my grandmother were to do all this, the words might look and feel very much like what Tasher has so expertly created here.

Tasher has helped thousands—if not tens of thousands—of separating and divorcing people with her divorce support website, Divorced and Scared No More. She has assembled the wisdom from those many years of supporting and listening into this series of books, carefully and extensively organized by subject matter, and is now hoping to help even more people though this maddening, suffocating, mind-numbing experience.

Having spent many years advising those in the middle of the disorienting world of divorce myself, I am thankful for her efforts because there are so few good references available to support people as they experience the difficulties of divorce. Tasher's books work together with her website, so readers can get personalized assistance.

The world would be a better place if the guy on the other side of the door you walk through when the divorce process begins handed each party a copy of Tasher's books. I suggest that former partners going through divorce give a copy of this series to close family and friends so each person's support group will also be well informed in the days and months ahead.

While my grandmother probably knew next to nothing about divorce (we never discussed it, and her generation had nowhere near today's 50 percent divorce rate), her connections in Heaven surely have brought together great wisdom and understanding. *Divorced and Scared No More!* may be the next best thing.

—William Kenly,
Author of *The Dogs of Divorce, The Dogs of Luck, The Dogs of Cancer, The Dogs of Business,* and *After the Diagnosis, Medullary Thyroid Cancer Memoirs*

Chapter 1

Lessons to Learn About Yourself

Plenty of things will happen in our lives due to our differences. Unfortunately, ending a relationship is sometimes unavoidable, and the transition from married to the single life is challenging. But if you do the work to heal and process your past, you will love again. Additionally, this love will be stronger than before because this time you will be better equipped to find the right person.

While you were married, you had somebody to discuss troubles and issues with; now you will need to solve everything on your own. At this time, you have to handle the worries of daily existence unaided, and then go home to a quiet house or possibly a noisy house with children to care for alone. It can even be challenging to experience an evening at home alone when are accustomed to sitting quietly alongside another person.

Eventually, though, most individuals find their way out of loneliness to the enjoyment of being alone. Once you enjoy your own company, you are ready to discover companionship in a new, healthy relationship.

Following the death of a marriage, each individual will be ready for dating at a different time. Relationship expert Tamsen Fadal recently said, "It's not a contest to see who gets out there first. You date when you are ready to get back out there and not before." Immediately after the official divorce procedures are over, feelings are running at high speed, and suffering people need a chance to heal before putting themselves back in the dating world.

Start dating by dating yourself first. Spend time repairing your self-esteem and taking the time to build up confidence in yourself. Pursue things you wanted to do either before or while you married but never had the time to try. Discover your desires and dreams (for more on finding your sense of self again after divorce, please see the first book in this series, *Divorced and Scared No More: Emotional Support for the Newly Divorced*). Take time to consider what your hopes are for any new relationship. Recognize all you have to offer another person, realizing why you are worthy of the best possible partner. You are a real catch, and you are lucky to have you. There will come a time when you will want to get back on the dating horse. But for now, it may be best to go horseback riding in real life as one of your new activities because the "dating horse" is wild, and it's easy to get thrown off.

There are many places you can visit on a date with yourself. At first, you may be worried people might notice you are alone, or you feel nervous about being alone. Go to an art gallery because most people walk alone from painting to painting with a glass of wine in their hands. Learn some art lingo though, so you can answer someone who may ask you about the non-organic, neo-surrealistic avant-garde style. Or go to a game dressed in the appropriate team-associated clothes, cap, and sunglasses. Get a hamburger, a refreshing drink, and enjoy yourself. Watch the game, yelling to your heart's content. Who knows, there might be another fan trying it on their own, and your presence could spark a flame. Getting out into the world again will also prepare you to not feel too awkward on your first date with another person.

With time, you will find yourself wanting to get back into dating again. You are beginning to open your heart, and hopefully, it will soon start to swell with love. Unfortunately, for many, there is also a little voice contemplating just what could fail. Say "Hello" to Mr. Nerves and his companion Ms. Jitters. They are so alike, they would probably be a couple by now, but they are both too afraid to ask each other out. They come to visit all of us at least once or twice. Acknowledge them and send them on their way.

Do You Love More?

In your past relationships, were there times when it seemed you put in so much more effort than your partner did? There may be some reasons why you attract partners who you love more than they love you. If any of these examples apply to you, there is a high likelihood you will end up with a partner just like your ex.

- *Did one or both of your parents fail to give you the love and attention you needed as a child?* You may believe that people don't love as deeply as you do. Because of this, you might have low self-esteem. Very often, people with low self-esteem attract partners who will validate their own critical opinion of themselves and not return love freely. You need to love yourself, acknowledge you are good enough and believe you deserve to be loved as deeply as you give love.
- *Did you grow up watching your parent always pursuing a partner?* You may have unconsciously concluded as a child that this is a "normal" type of relationship. We usually repeat the lessons we learned as children. Remember, as mentioned in the second book in the series *Practical Advice for the Newly Divorced* observational learning occurs through

observing negative and positive behaviors. At an early age, a child learns to use observational learning skills in multiple spheres of life. Observational learning differs from imitative learning in that it does not require a duplication of the behavior exhibited by the parent. For example, the child may observe an unwanted behavior and the subsequent consequences, and thus learn to refrain from that behavior. But if they think this is normal, they will repeat the action they have learned. Take time and teach your children well, so they will learn how to have healthy and fulfilling relationships. Understand it is not healthy to give love and not be entitled to receive love. You need to break this cycle not only for you but for your children as well. We all have an emptiness that needs filling from time to time when it comes to love and happiness.

- *Did your parents have the perfect storybook relationship?* Many grew up with parents who were in sync regarding almost every issue life threw at them. At times it may have felt like they shared one brain. Children who never see their parents disagree and view their parents as the perfect couple. Often they compare any relationship, they have to what they "thought" their parents had. Unfortunately, no one can live up to the standard of perfection that you saw through the eyes of childhood.

No matter what the reason is for being in this type of relationship, the results will be the same: You will end up feeling hungry for love, lonely, angry, and cheated. With professional help, you can heal the wounds of your past and learn how to build a healthy relationship. Learn what the warning signs are and watch for them. Don't fall into the trap of making excuses for your partner about why he or she can't love you the way you want and deserve.

Is It Possible to Find Love Again?

After a divorce, many people ask, "Is it possible to find love again?" Finding love after divorce is always possible. You may not feel that way right now, but you bought this book, so you are well on your way. As the minister at my church said, "When you are going through the valley of changing or troubled times, keep walking. The only ones stuck are the ones that stop walking." Yes, healing a broken heart and trusting another person again can be a challenge. Your heart and mind may build up strong walls. You are doing this to protect yourself, but it can make you feel like you are getting nowhere. There is always at least some type of damage after a divorce. The divorce rate is on the rise, and as a result, there are more and more of us out there looking for new love.

If you are looking to find love again, there are a few things that can help you succeed. Here are your first two steps to help get you on the path to finding a strong, healthy, happy relationship.

- **Let go of your anger:** Even when you try to hide your animosity, and you believe no one else knows, others do. When you are holding onto all the negative feelings, just the mention of your ex's name and you will display what is called "a tell" in a poker game. Even if you think they don't people do see it. It is natural to feel skeptical after losing a relationship, but when people cannot let go of the bitterness, they start to build a wall around themselves. Negativity, sarcasm, and other signs of being bitter are written all over their faces. The people you are trying to attract will not want to be around you if they sense this bitterness. But the essential reason to shed your anger is that it will make you feel so much better when you do. Free yourself, and you will smile more, breathe easier, and have a lot more fun.

- **Acceptance:** I know you have heard this; I sure did, many, many times. A divorce is like a death. You need to mourn the death of your relationship. You will grieve because all the hopes and dreams you had with this partner will never come true. You need to do this even if you were the one who initiated the divorce. Skipping the grieving process will never work in the long run. You can get into a relationship that is all wrong and end up hurting yourself more. Some people exercise, go to therapy, take yoga, and read to help themselves feel better. For more practical ideas about life after divorce, see the second book in this series, *Divorced and Scared No More: Practical Advice for the Newly Divorced*. Our church, as well as many other churches, has a divorce workshop to help people. You need to find a way that is best for you during this process. When you have finally healed yourself, then you are ready to start to look for love.

Remember, there is a necessary time to heal and move on after a divorce. You need to take positive steps so that you can begin another exciting and significant chapter in your life. Having a failed relationship in the past should not prevent you from pursuing the possibilities of finding a new life partner and creating much better relationships.

Dating after Divorce

The Deeper the Hole, the Higher the Building

I heard somebody say

*T*he deeper the hole, the higher the building,

*S*o I dug down deep in my soul,

*A*nd I dug with a heart unyielding.

*P*enetrating the dirt

*R*ight where I stood,

I scooped up the hurt

*O*nly poor me could.

*R*eady to raise myself up

*I*nto what had been drawn on paper,

*T*he foundation of a person

*Y*ou'd see as a skyscraper.

—*Tony Haynes*

Learn to enjoy your own company.
Others will follow suite.

Chapter 2

Prepare Yourself to Date

Are You Ready to Take the Plunge?

Divorce isn't the end of ever having an excellent relationship. But having undergone the tedious process of moving on after a divorce can intimidate someone who's thinking of entering the dating world again. However, it is essential to remember not to date until you are ready to do so, no matter what anyone tells you. Surely you want your next relationship to be a success, so you need to understand where you are in the healing process.

Give yourself some time to heal. Make sure you firmly hammered the past in your history, along with any hurt, bitterness, and baggage from a failed marriage. Only when you fully understand what went wrong in your relationship. What part you played in the collapse of your marriage will you be able to identify what makes a good relationship. If you understand and have accomplished the tasks in this section, it is time, and you are ready to give love a second chance. Otherwise, you might set yourself up for more disappointment and pain.

Some clues to tell that you are now ready to take the plunge into the dating world again after divorce:

- **You are prepared to start dating when you are excited at the prospect of meeting people.** You are not ready to date when thinking about meeting people makes you tremble. Or if you still do not find even the slightest excitement at the prospect of meeting people. You are ready to start dating again when you begin to think dating is an exciting adventure where you can have fun meeting new people.
- **When you can identify what you want, what you don't want, and what other standards you expect from your next partner, you are now a step closer to dating again**. Coming from a failed marriage, you probably want your future relationship to be with a partner who has few similarities with your ex-partner. But wait: what about someone who shares some of your ex-partners good qualities? After all, your ex-lover wasn't bad throughout the marriage. There were reasons that person was in your life. They were right for you at one time, and they were what you needed at that time. Remember to treat each

prospect individually, try to get to know each one better. Identify their good traits because it is wrong to compare an ex-partner to any potential opportunities you meet.

- **When you begin to feel neutral about your ex-partner, that's a sign; you are ready to start dating.** Having been in a relationship with your ex-partner for some time, it is natural during and after a divorce to still have some good feelings toward your ex-spouse. After a divorce is over, many have positive emotions such as fondness, but not necessarily love, for their ex-spouses.

On the other hand, you may still be harboring anger or homicidal feelings toward your ex-partner. When you begin to feel neutral about your ex-partner—that is, you can think of them without feeling angry, irritated, homicidal, or wistful—then you are good to go at taking another plunge into the dating world.

- **When you enjoy your own company and feel it is okay to be alone, it is the right time to start dating.** I can tell you firsthand that the early days after a divorce are terrifying, isolating, and lonely. It is very hard at first when you are used to being in a relationship, to now find yourself going it alone. It stinks. But once you learn how to be comfortable being by yourself after divorce, you get a gift: an empowering, independent feeling that brings reflection, self-love, self-confidence, and most of all, peace. There is a big difference between being alone and being lonely. You need to understand the difference between those two words before you begin to date. I feel the divorce rate on second (or later) marriages would be lower if people took the time to be comfortable being alone. People also need to understand how to deal with feelings of loneliness. People who take the time to deal with these feelings are more likely to find the right person and not to rush into a doomed relationship. The urgency to not be alone isn't necessary. If you enjoy your own company, others will, too.

Ways to Feel Dateable While Happily Divorced

Being happily divorced doesn't necessarily mean that you feel up to the challenge of dating again. Being used to a particular way of life for so long may have left you feeling comfortable and with certain expectations about relationships. Now that your comfort zone is gone, you may feel insecure about getting back into dating. These feelings are very natural in divorce recovery, and you're not the first person to experience them.

Instead, it is the chance to rediscover who you are outside of your marriage; your identity may have been wrapped up with your partner so much that you forgot you're a separate person. Going through a divorce shatters that reality, and you have to reconstruct your image from the ground up. Accomplish a few things and move yourself to a happily divorced state before you begin to date.

- **Become sexually confident:** Post-divorce, it's crucial that you reexamine what makes you feel alive again to regain your self-confidence. An activity you enjoy, whether it's going out to bars or dancing in clubs, even by yourself, is an excellent distraction from the stress of divorce and strengthens you as you cope with divorce depression. It's also a chance for you to be involved in activities that ex-spouse may not have enjoyed or didn't want to participate in because they didn't like it. It is about doing what you love and helping yourself heal before you're ready to start dating again.

- **Build a new social circle:** As a married couple, you and your ex-spouse may have built a circle of friends who had similar interests. In moving on from divorce, however, you may find that your friends have taken sides, essentially splitting the circle between you and your ex-partner. Set some time aside to introduce new people into your life, those who have no connection to your ex. Not only will this eliminate any unsolicited advice you want to avoid, but it will also give you a clean slate to work with when finding potential dates.

- **Reinvent your wardrobe:** There is little expectation to look sexy all the time for your spouse during your marriage. Not doing so may have left your wardrobe looking a bit outdated or even shabby. Give yourself a new look so that you transform yourself from divorced to happily divorced. You don't want your dates to get the impression that you're still suffering from the effects of your marriage ending. Changing your image creates a positive atmosphere around you, and you'll feel more positive internally and improve your chances of coping with divorce depression. If your budget isn't up to scratch, it never hurts to try on clothes that accentuate the best parts of you, even if you don't plan on buying them. Anything that brightens your day and your attitude is a step closer in moving on from divorce.

- **New lingerie, please. Donate your old pajamas:** Do you want to wear old things when you do find someone new? Just picture this: Your new partner says he likes your little nighty, and you respond, "Thanks, my ex loved this one, too!" There probably won't be any fireworks then—at least not the kind you would enjoy.

Being divorced may seem like a heavy burden to carry around with you, but the sooner you shrug it off, the better. Remember, it is a continuation of your opportunity to start over and rediscover yourself. There's no need to rush the process of finding the right person to have in your life.

Where to Find Love

When a divorced person is in a comfortable, healthy place and ready to find love, there are right ways, and there are wrong ways to start looking for it. There will still be old scars, and a bad experience may deal you a tremendous setback. Internet dating sites, matchmaker companies, singles bars, or the pressure of blind dates can prove to be too much for a divorced person at first. With time, you will get there, but until then, here are some ideas

You can start by meeting new friends while volunteering, joining singles groups at a church, or joining social groups like one on meetup.com. Joining a new group will increase the likelihood of finding people with shared interests and will boost your self-esteem. It is time to get back into the world once more and find the love you seek because it is unlikely to find you if you sit at home.

Online dating can be a useful tool, and there are services like "It's Just Lunch," which does have a screening process and can provide background checks. With both of these types of services, be honest in all aspects when it comes to describing who you are and what you want. The more accurate you are, the better your chances of finding the right person.

Finding love after a divorce is possible, but please try to take a slow, comfortable pace. The key to finding love again is to make sure you take time to grieve and heal before beginning the search. You need to be truly ready to date to avoid having negative experiences or attracting the wrong people. When you feel ready, it should be at a slow pace, in a positive environment.

The Most Common Dating Blunders to Avoid

You are single again; the divorce is final, and chances are you have already decided to take the plunge into the dating world. However, you should be careful not to make dating an escape or a means to get over the pain of your previous ordeal. If you do that, you are not moving on but only masking the genuine emotions deep inside of you. You should only start a new relationship when you have already moved on from the past because only then can you be ready to commit to another person again.

As you take the plunge into the dating world again after a divorce, you may find yourself making the same dating mistakes over and over and over again. These are some of the most common dating mistakes committed. It is essential to recognize and understand them so that you will avoid repeating them in your next dates. If you commit to avoiding these mistakes, your chances of having a great relationship with a new partner can be significantly improved.

- **Holding onto past baggage:** All of us have been hurt in the past and has undergone one of the most painful ordeals, divorce, you have accumulated the emotional baggage that you might be unaware of you have it. To increase your chances of having a committed relationship with a new partner, you should stop holding onto the pains of your past relationship. It is now time to unload this emotional baggage so that you won't get stuck with it.
    - o If you have not done so already, it is about time to begin an internal dialogue with yourself and spend enough time alone to examine what led to the collapse of your marriage. While you may tend to blame your ex-partner, ask yourself if you have had any destructive habits, too. The fact that you are blaming others is already an indication that you have a destructive pattern. Rather than blaming others for

the way you feel, start owning your feelings. For instance, instead of saying, "You are making me angry," it is a lot better to say, "The way you acted doesn't feel so good, and it's making me uncomfortable."

- o Avoiding blame or pursuing other destructive habits is a way to differentiate your new relationship. Try to reflect on what you can do to make this relationship work because only then can you unload your baggage and welcome an excellent relationship into your life. Anyone who has lived life has baggage, and that's okay. It is how people deal with the baggage that may be the problem. Learn how to deal with your baggage properly and constructively; do not let your baggage control you.

- **Comparing all prospective partners to your ex:** Having been hurt in a previous relationship makes trusting a new person difficult. However, if you don't eliminate your distrust, then trusting potential partners may be impossible and can destroy your chances of building a new, fulfilling relationship. Given your experience, you will likely think that all prospects are like your ex-partner (for instance, you might think that they are cheaters and can easily fall out of love if that's what happened with your previous partner). Treat each person individually and try to find out all the ways your new partner is very different from your ex. Seek out the good qualities in your new lover and give yourself a chance to know him or her better by starting with a clean slate.

- **Approaching first and share flirting:** In my view, after divorce, most people are struggling to get back into the rhythm of dating and may have commitment issues. An excellent way to make contact with someone you are interested in is to smile or say, "Hello." No matter how attracted you are to that person, it is better to wait for the other person to make the next move after showing them that you are interested in them. With this understated approach, you allow the other person to take it from there, allowing both of you to participate equally in flirting.

- **Quickly jumping into a whirlwind romance:** As they say, people can fall out of love as quickly as they fall in love. It can be such a wonderful and flattering feeling if someone you just met takes time to see you many times a week and spends long hours talking to you over the phone. From there, you might find yourself entering into the relationship quickly. Unfortunately, as sudden as it comes, the hot romance in this scenario suddenly fizzles out and burns up fast. Give adequate time to get to know the person before committing to a relationship. There is no problem in dating more than one person at a time, as long as all parties involved know an exclusive relationship is not on the table yet.

- **Deciding to marry too soon:** Another common dating mistake committed is the decision to marry a new partner after less than a year in the relationship. Rushing into marriage is not a good move. Very often, it is committed by people who want to replace their old relationships with new ones. For some of these people, any warm-blooded body will do. Very often, these people haven't yet completed their healing process and do not know how to enjoy being alone.
    o Many people put their best foot forward in the first year of a relationship. They try their best not to show their flaws. In the second year, flaws from both of you will start coming out, and by the third year, you will see what you will get in the long run. The best advice is to take the time to know each other well before deciding to get married. In the process, you will start becoming more committed in your exclusive dating relationship.
- **Being overly chummy:** How would you feel if you just met a person, and they started telling you about a guy they had an altercation with at their office, or a fight with their brother, or all the details of a new root canal? Remember that during the early stage of dating, you are virtually strangers, so it is not good to share some intimate details about your life. Doing so would make you look desperate and worst, neurotic. The more you talk about yourself, the more time

you lose to observe the other person and to learn if they are right for you. Just relax and enjoy your time together. Do not make the mistake of impressing them with too much witty banter or enumerating your accomplishments. Being overly friendly will turn off your date.

If you are serious about becoming successful in your next relationship after divorce, avoid these blunders at all costs. Perhaps the only way to be happy again is to make sure that you are prepared to enter a new relationship and that you are ready to forget the past. Avoiding these mistakes can lead you to better relationships. If you do not want to end up suffering from the same pitfalls over again, change your ways, and do not be in such a hurry to get into a new relationship. Stay away from headache and stress due to another broken relationship by avoiding the most common dating mistakes listed above.

Dating Is a Time to Have Fun and Meet New People

Dating is a **time to have fun** and meet new people. It should not be the express lane to your next relationship or marriage. View each date as an opportunity to find out more about what you do and do not want in a future partner. Accept as many dates as you want, but remember that a date is just a date. It's only one evening of your life, and if you don't hit it off or you do not go out with the person again, it is okay. There is always tomorrow, and good things come to those who wait. Unless your first date is genuinely awful, give her or him another chance on a second date. Many people are nervous on first dates and do not always make a good first impression.

Do not show up with a checklist or think too deeply on the first date. Just enjoy each other's company and try to get to know each other's likes and dislikes. The only decision about the future is whether or not you would like to see the person for a second date. That decision does not need to be made until the date is over. Keep the date light and fun. Information about past relationships should be banned on first dates. There is nothing fun about hearing about another person's mistreatment by an ex and subsequent heartbreak. I have listened to details about things from the ex-wife's plastic surgery to fights over frozen embryos. That was an odd conversation, but I did learn a little about how people deal with those little embryos. If a date starts down that road, either I find another topic they are interested in or excuse myself and go to the restroom. When I get back, I bring up something else to discuss.

Not a social butterfly? That's okay!

You are not a social butterfly, and that is just fine. Start dating in a way that makes you feel comfortable. Here are some suggestions that will help you navigate the dating world if you are introverted.

- **Fess up.** Do not pretend to be a social butterfly—there is nothing wrong with being introverted. Tell your date if you are someone who seeks friendship first or needs time to fall in love. Doing this, you may scare away a few of the flakes and instead attract people who will understand and like you.

- **Meet at a location where you feel comfortable.** If you don't like loud places, don't go to them. Often introverts are also "pleasers," and they will do what is asked of them even if they suffer. Find a place that makes you feel comfortable and go for it.
- **Avoid smooth talkers.** If your date won't allow you to get a word in edgewise, he or she is not the right person for you, so move on.
- **Soft connections.** Sometimes we get so flooded by first impressions and things to look out for that it's difficult to feel what it's like to just sit with a person. Do you like being there? Does being with your date feel crowded; do you feel overwhelmed, or nervous? Make sure you enjoy being with your date.
- **Beware of takers.** Introverts are often givers. They listen, pay attention, and want to be there for the other person. Make sure you get to be on the receiving end of the equation. If it's all about them on the dates, chances are, in a relationship they would expect the same—and more.

Is It Okay to Date More Than One Person?

When I was young, if a boy liked a girl, he asked her on a date. If the girl was also interested in him, she would accept the invitation. For some reason, we were expected to continue seeing each other and to try to make a relationship work. I know many people still practice this type of dating ritual, and many others married the wrong person because of it. Just because you went out for coffee does not mean that your date is the right person for you. There is nothing wrong with dating more than one person at a time.

People have asked me, "How can you date more than one person at a time?" The answer to that question is simple: "I am just dating, and I am not in a romantic relationship with anyone. We enjoy one another's company; our dating is non-exclusive and platonic." While dating after my divorce, I wanted to be discerning, have a keen mental perception, vision, and understanding in my dating. The word that sums all those attributes up is **perspicacious** [pur-spi-key-shuh s]. It is time to learn a new word and a new way to date. Dating is one phase, and a relationship is another—they are not the same thing. Unfortunately, many have blended these two phases or skipped the dating phase entirely.

Regularly, many well-meaning people have let me know I should date one man at a time and give him a "chance." Some have gone so far as to tell me it was the "Christian" thing to do. These well-meaning people do not understand that we not only are giving each other a chance to be friends; we are also learning from each other about life in general and about ourselves.

I have not found any written rules in my faith that have told me how to date. There are some guidelines about what not to do while dating; for instance, dating a married person is absolutely not permitted. The guidelines of your faith are essential to follow because your faith is part of your personality. Therefore, your deal breakers are a must to understand while dating. But who says just because you went on a date or two, you have to date only that person? Dating is a time to explore what your desires and feelings are. It is just an opportunity to share your time and make new friends. This is especially true after a divorce. You must take the time to learn about yourself so you can find the partner who fulfills you.

God puts people in our paths for different reasons. Some will help you look within yourself and discover your true feelings or views. I have found this to be true for me because I did not realize how many of my beliefs were based on what others told me were the "proper" beliefs. Because of some of the men I have dated, they opened my eyes to what my actual views are. Thankfully, sometimes I have been able to watch and learn, by their example, how to deal with my ex. Some of the gentlemen I socialize with remind me to take a break from my endless to-do list and go out and have fun. Then I have met a few men who weren't right for me, but who have been just perfect for a friend of mine to date. If I had not been a perspicacious dater, these couples might not have gotten together, or if they had, it might have become an uncomfortable situation.

Take your time and enjoy dating. Learn about yourself and what will fulfill you. Join groups like MeetUp.com and get to know many new people with the same interests. Do this as the next phase after healing, and rushing into a relationship could destroy so much of the hard work you have done. Dating is just a time to socialize with others while learning about yourself.

Emotional Attraction Is Stronger than Physical
Remember, It's Not Easy Being Green

I met Devin one day in the clubhouse at the golf course. He was amusing, and I thoroughly enjoyed his company. The more I got to know him, the more interested I became. For me, the emotional attraction is what typically makes a person more physically attractive to me. A man's personality is what I am attracted to, and if they make me laugh, they are on the fast track to physical attraction.

The night after the election in November 2012, we had a social gathering with several friends from the neighborhood. As the conversation turned to the election, Devin started telling us his father is black, and he voted for the president because he is half black. I, like many others at the gathering, was surprised because Devin is light-skinned and has blue-green hazel eyes.

I have many relatives who have married outside of their race, but I had a foolish knee-jerk reaction. The next time I saw Devin, I told him it would be better being only friends until I learned how to deal with my problem. I also told him that I didn't understand why I even had this problem and didn't know I did until the previous week. I have many people in my life who are of various races, but I just had never dated someone from a different race, and I needed time to sit down and sort out my feelings. He was not upset at all and seemed to understand, but he did say, "I cannot change my race or mixed race any more than you can change your eye color from being green."

I took some time, and I thought about what he had said. At the next gathering, I noticed he had started flirting with another woman. Yes, I did get jealous, and I realized he was right: I could not change my eye color any more than he could change his race, or I could change my race. He was and is the same man he was the day I met him. He had changed nothing; I was the person with the flaw. I always knew God had made us all the same. In every other aspect of my life, I dealt with racial or any other issues that way. Why did I look at dating for myself differently?

It was Christmas time, and as I walked up to my Christmas tree holding a beautifully wrapped present, I realized we as humans are just like these presents. There were presents wrapped in red, green, blue, and white paper with a whole mixture of colors. That is what race is; it's the wrapping paper on our bodies. God made us with different wrapping paper on the outside. Since we are just like those presents when it comes to a person, what does it matter what color their skin, eyes, hair, religion, or age is?

I sat down and wanted to review why I reacted the way I did to this man. Then I realized two significant people in my life were very prejudiced against various races and religions. These two people were my abusers, and without realizing it, even though I had removed them from my life, I was still allowing them to control my thoughts and actions. I had allowed their views to stay with me, and now, it was time to remove them. I had to start to identify the beliefs that were not my own and learn to take them out of my life one at a time. They no longer control my views or actions on anything; it was time for my own beliefs to guide me.

I started thinking more about those presents. When Christmas day comes, we will open all the presents, and most of us will

discard the wrapping paper and remove it from our lives. We keep the gifts that were inside the wrapping paper. When dating, look at what's on the inside of the person and not at the wrapping paper. If you continue to look only at the wrapping paper, you may miss one of the greatest gifts God has to offer. This person may be the puzzle piece that's the perfect fit with yours, the one piece that can complete your **puzzle called life.** Keep in mind that just as you may have to get past their wrapping paper, they may be struggling to get past your wrapping paper too.

Devin and I have continued to date, and as time passed, I realized he also struggles with issues from his past relationships. Often, he assumes that because I am a woman, I must fit into the same category and react the same as other women he's dated. But after I shared with him my struggle due to race, he realized he was struggling similarly with gender bias. Now we both view race and gender as the wrapping paper, and we are grateful that we are puzzle pieces in each other's lives.

Single Again and Dating with Children

Dating is tough, but in many ways, it is more difficult for those who are divorced. Combined with the fears of being out of practice, there are often children's feelings to take into consideration. How can a single parent enjoy a new romance without lying awake during the night, worrying about doing emotional harm to their children?

I have heard many say they are going to use this time to focus on their children instead of dating. Who was focusing on the children while these people were married or getting the divorce? If you have children, you should always focus on them. Dating will not distract you from focusing on your children unless you don't budget your time correctly. Remember the kids' time is their time, which means it is time to disconnect and unplug (no texting, Facebook, or email). One of the best things you can do for your children right now is to take the time to rebuild yourself. Not only will you be improving the quality of life for all of you, but the children are being taught by your example of how to cope after something bad happens in life. Many people take this time and pursue things they wanted to do either before or while they were married but never had the time to do. You may be in a rough time psychologically, but this will enable you to discover your desires and dreams. It is time to re-develop a sense of self and choose what you like to have in your life. It truly is a new beginning and the time to consider what your hopes are for any new relationship.

Dating after divorce may feel strange. Go out to enjoy the date and have a good time. You never know it may lead to romance, or you may not click, but you won't know until you go. You're single now, and your life is full of opportunities. Don't stay home dwelling on the past. Get out there and give that date a go. You will be surprised that dating after divorce can bring about positive results. Have fun and then go out and have some more fun. Make sure to keep repeating this process until you find that someone special and never stop having fun and enjoying your life.

Oprah Radio host Rabbi Shmuley says, "Bring your children into the process. Explain to them why it's important you date, and reassure them no person will ever take their place." It is advisable to date in a respectful manner as well as an understanding of your children's needs, emotions, and thoughts. His "Rules for Dating after Divorce" were created to ensure your new relationship and your children flourish.

You are not betraying anyone by trying to be happy, but you do need to consider your children when you are dating. Especially when you have children, please do not go for the flavor of the week and bring an endless trail of brand-new people into their lives. Remember, they are learning from your actions. Do you want them to grow up and be bringing the flavor of the week to visit you?

Your child has one mother and one father; having your children refer to a new partner as "Mommy" or "Daddy" will not only make them feel as if they are betraying their other parent but also confuse young children. Also, what if the relationship does not last? Just how many "daddies" and "mommies" are going to be introduced into your child's life? The same goes for using the terms "Uncle" or "Aunt" when referring to the new partner. If the relationship ends, the children will feel families can and will quickly desert them, which is a very unhealthy attitude.

Many people ask me how much time an individual should wait before introducing a new boyfriend or girlfriend to their children. No matter how excited you are to meet someone new, do not make the mistake of introducing the new person into your kids' lives too soon. Just like you and your ex, your kids are also in an episode of darkness, seeing their parents going in separate ways. If you date a person for a short time, introduce that person to the children, and then the relationship ends, the children will feel a sense of abandonment. No child should be subjected to this after experiencing divorce. Therefore, I do not think anyone who is not a serious partner should be introduced to your children. You are not deceiving them; instead, you are taking the time to find someone who has true partner potential.

Children need time to heal, as well. If the new partner doesn't respect that, he or she is undoubtedly not good potential partner material. For many relationships, the initial three months is the honeymoon period. Things are all fresh and exciting. After about six months, the happy couple tends to relax, and the "good behavior" will begin to disappear. Then people obtain a peek at the person actual personality. Before deciding to introduce the individual, you are dating to the children; you will want to discover what their goals are. Determine if the person's values and beliefs are consistent with yours, and establish a friendship with him or her.

Here are a couple of ideas regarding how to introduce a new partner to your children, and both start with *not* introducing them as your new partner. Hopefully, you have friends of the opposite sex in your daily life who your children know and interact with often. If this is the case, it is a fantastic idea to introduce your brand-new partner as merely another one of your friends. When your group gets together, incorporate your new partner. Your children will view them as somebody new in the group.

Perhaps the new partner also has children. Arrange an afternoon when you and yours "run into" them and theirs at the park. It can be a relaxed way for everyone involved to get to know each other. Possibly plan to meet at the park every week, but start taking a picnic basket.

Whichever approach you decide upon, slowly allow the relationship to evolve; there is no timetable, and it is far better to let the relationship develop naturally with the children. Keep including your new partner in more activities as time goes by. When sufficient time has passed, talk to your children and let them know you are interested in this person and ask how they would feel if the new person became your boyfriend or girlfriend. You are not giving the children veto power, but you are allowing the children to express their feelings regarding the idea of you dating the person. If they say they would hate it, encourage them to reveal the reasons why. Some children may still be holding on to the dream that Mommy and Daddy will get back together. If you know why they are hesitant for you to date the person, tackle those issues before the two of you officially date in front of the children. Once again, if professional help is needed, please seek this out because you could be sparing your child a lifetime of poor relationship practices.

Colored by White Light

*Y*ou don't see color; you see
*E*very soul colored by white light.
*A*nd if you
*H*eld a crayon in your hand,

*Y*ou would color
*E*very face with purple polka dots
*A*nd yellow sunny smiles that
*H*ide the hate in man.

*Y*ou don't see a difference; you see
*E*vidence of God who lives within:
A colorful
*H*uman being ...
 Regardless of the color of their skin.
 —Tony Haynes

A perspicacious dater understands no one is perfect on a first date including themselves.

Chapter 3

Be a Perspicacious Dater

Four Types of Dating Strategies

In this new dating world, I have found four types of dating strategies. We have "They Showed Me Attention," "Checklists," "Serial Daters," or "Perspicacious Daters."

Someone Showed Me Attention

These daters are attracted to anyone who shows attention and asks them on a date, and many believe they must try to explore only that person until they determine if there is a possibility for a relationship.

Maybe it is because of my age, but this strategy was not acceptable to me.

I am over fifty, so time could be a problem if I were required to spend three to six months with a person to *"see if"* we might be compatible in a relationship. How long will it take before I learn what I want in a relationship? Do I have enough years left to figure it out and then find someone who fulfills me? How do you end what now has become a relationship without hurting the person, and is it possible to continue a friendship? What if I had said "no" to a date with the right man while dating the wrong one—could I ever find him again? With the days and years going by faster and faster, I didn't want to take any chances with those questions.

Just a simple touch or smile when someone has not received one for months or years may make them faint, or it may be mistaken for a potential relationship application. Feeling starved for attention daters, become attached to the first person who shows them affection. Unfortunately, some people realize how vulnerable people feel after a divorce and will use it to their advantage to achieve their goals. They will probably not give a second thought to you and your feelings. It does not matter why these types of relationships start, but they usually end quickly. If you do not learn why you are attracted to people instantly, the process will be repeated again and again, leading to a string of relationships that are unhealthy and not fulfilling to the heart.

In most cases, the divorced person probably has a self-defeating thought pattern. Just going through a divorce reinforces these thought patterns. Charles Edward Sherman and Warren Farrell, authors of *Make Any Divorce Better,* point out that because of these psychological traps many people *unintentionally* increase their anguish as well as lengthen it. The self-defeating thought patterns keep you stuck in anger, anxiety, or depression. Numerous thoughts are hindering your capability to move forward and finding a fulfilling relationship, such as:

- "I'm likely to end up alone forever because there are not any real, honest ones left." (You're real and honest, and that proves there is one and there are many more just like you.)
- "I'm too old, my body isn't what it used to be. I'm fat. I'm ugly." (So you don't look like you did when you were in your teens, but some of those extra pounds may have made some pretty lovely curves. So what if you are balding? Shave it off; there are some women, like me, who prefer bald men.)
- "There just are not enough normal people to pick from; therefore, I must settle for whoever shows interest in me." (Seriously though, what does it mean to be normal? You find me a normal person, and I will find you a rainbow-colored, bad-tempered unicorn wearing braces and a toupée. Neither one exists.)
- "What if I get too seriously involved with someone and out of the blue my ex parachutes in and wants me back?"

(Honestly, if you still have this hope, you're not ready for a new relationship. This train of thought will most likely create a subconscious barrier. Whether you realize it or not, you are comparing any potential mates to your ex and still wearing those rose-colored glasses.)

- "I do not deserve a good partner." (You deserve the best that life has to offer you!)

As you see, these statements and others like them are just based on fear. There are two types of fear: the first is anxiety about being alone, and the other is being nervous about possible rejection. Many divorced people jump into relationships prematurely merely because they are afraid of being alone. Doing so is indeed an error in judgment. Frequently, with this attitude, you will have a panicked feeling, just like you are marching into battle to obtain the last eligible person on the planet (Unfortunately, people think of dating as war. I wonder if that is why they are always dressed to kill). Doing so will lead to settling for a relationship that is just not fulfilling or even as functional as you deserve. You might remain with someone you may very well not have even given a second's consideration to if you hadn't merely feared to be alone.

Settling for less should not be an option, even if the person under consideration is the last single person left. (In the event of a worldwide Armageddon, where every human being gets wiped out except for you and this one other single person, you still need to be sensibly selective between taking the one or remaining single; but now we are venturing into a different self-help book with zombies in it.)

Make an effort to look at being alone in a very new light. Consider yourself as liberated to live your life filled with friends, hobbies, and free to pursue all of your dreams. Date freely platonically and do not settle for anyone less than you deserve. If you have the right perspective regarding single life, you will not panic so easily.

The fear of being rejected by a potential partner can become so paralyzing that some end up spending the rest of their lives alone. People may shy away from relationships simply because they do not feel adequate, deserving, or just because they do not know how to handle being rejected. Unfortunately, these people are likely to end up in relationships that are less than what they would like and deserve. It might be ok for a short time, but the emptiness will set in again, and they will find themselves alone.

Expect rejection and don't take it to heart; accept that the person who rejected you wasn't the right person for you and move on. Not everyone is right for you, just as you are not right for everyone. With each day and each step, it will get easier to overcome the fear of rejection.

Deal Breakers versus Checklists

In the world of dating, people have been encouraged to create checklists when looking for a potential partner. These lists can quickly become endless and more often than not, unrealistic. Most of us are relatively ordinary people. The failed checklist system is something no one, including you or me, can live up to achieving. These lists seem to take on a life of their own while they grow and grow, becoming more and more impractical to the point that no human can even partially fulfill the list. The checklists I have seen all include *"No baggage."* If you have lived your life and are divorced, you have baggage, and so does any potential partner you may find.

We are all pretty much average, yet many of these lists have so much to do with physical features, although the physical attraction in a relationship will soon fade. An emotional attraction can grow into a powerful physical attraction. One day you might find yourself kissing those *"Dumbo Ears"* goodnight, realizing they are one of your partner's most attractive qualities, and recognizing God gave them to this person so they can really listen to you, better than your ex ever did.

No one should change or be changed to have a relationship. Unfortunately, many believe they ought to concentrate on the good aspects of a potential partner and overlook any tiny way in which they are not compatible. Others take overlooking differences a step further and do not communicate to the new partner about how they are feeling. The notion of picking your battles is an essential part of the way you approach conflict in marriage because there will almost always be some disagreements, regardless of how compatible the couple is. However, it is not the method you should use when you are trying to select a partner and build a new relationship.

The courting period is the time to discover your compatibility as partners; it is not the time to hide your true feelings or start making mental notes about the things you will change concerning your partner when you are in a much more serious relationship. Just as you wish people would "let me be myself," let them be themselves so everyone can shine with their own life. Rachel Sussman, the author of *The Break-Up Bible,* writes, "If you notice red flags and still go forward, hoping for someone to change or for a different outcome, you are setting yourself up for a bad breakup." When a person makes a change, for it to become a permanent change, they must desire the change for themselves. If a change is made for any other reason, it may last for a short time, but any changes made solely to make someone else happy are rarely permanent.

Remember, nobody is perfect, including you. Well, Morgan Freeman (God in *Bruce Almighty* and *Evan Almighty*) and Sally Field (she was the *Flying Nun* after all) are perfect, and James Earl Jones and Vin Diesel have perfect voices. But mostly, we have flaws. Sometimes those odd little quirks could turn out to be the thing you love most about your partner.

Relationships are never perfect; they all require compromise. The proverbial line-in-the-sand deal breakers are specific issues that are simply non-negotiable. You should only have about four or five—anymore, and you will be creating a checklist, and we just talked about those.

To give you an idea of how deal-breakers are different from a checklist, I will share mine.

1. My relationship with God is very important to me. My partner does not have to share my beliefs, but I need him to support my feelings.
2. I cannot be involved with a person connected with drug use or someone addicted to gambling. If they have an addiction, our relationship will never come first.
3. I cannot date a person if they have ever cheated or abused anyone in any way (physical, emotional, verbal, or sexual). It does not matter what the circumstances were; to me, these things can never be justified.
4. I need to be physically and emotionally attracted to a man. Having poor hygiene or appearance stops the physical attraction immediately. On the other side of the coin, an emotionally attractive man can become physically attractive over time.

All humans are naturally flawed; expecting a person to be perfect is not only unrealistic but will also most likely lead to disappointment and loneliness. As you establish your list of deal-breakers, keep in mind your goal is not to try to find the perfect human being but to find the person who is ideal for you, bringing out the best in both of you. Overlooking or finding traits you would like to change about the person should never be a part of your dating experience. The divorce courts are full of cases where people went into the marriage with those attitudes, and yours may have been one of them.

When you find someone who seems to be ideal except for a particular mannerism, ask yourself: "What makes me think I have the right to change another person to whatever suits me? What makes me think I am so suitable? Do I live in a bubble of a superiority delusion of 'I am the professor, and my spouse is my pupil'?" Pop your bubble, friend; the intention is not to slaughter someone's soul with marriage unless you want an unhappy marriage or another divorce.

There is no "I" in relationship—well, maybe in the spelling, but not in the bonds of two people living and sharing in perfect harmony.

Serial Daters

Also known as players, serial daters methodically date an obscene number of individuals in a short period of time. For example, they might have half a dozen or more dates with different individuals within a week. Many view dating as a sport. They do not view it as a means to find out more about themselves and what they are looking for in a mate. They are noncommittal, and nothing is amusing about dating a real non-committal person.

There are two types of serial daters, and both are often insecure and have low self-esteem. They need another person to give them attention and to make them feel good about themselves. The first type of serial dater lines up as many dates as possible with multiple partners. They choose not to focus on one person. No homework or filtering is done; they are just out for a casual good time. Maybe they are looking for self-fulfillment or an ego boost. Perhaps they are just looking for sex.

I once knew a guy who would go into a bar, walk up to women, and say, "You want to go home with me?" Nine out of ten times he would get his face slapped, but the tenth time he would get what he was looking for, and the game was on. He was the extreme example of a serial dater. Most serial daters either aren't looking for anything in particular, or they are looking for something specific. They jump from date to date, and if they don't find that one thing they want— ego boost, sex, the Fourth-of-July-fireworks spark—they immediately move on to the next date.

The second type of serial dater is the type who feels they always need a boyfriend or girlfriend. This type of serial dater believes they are in love after the first or second date. Relationships like this usually last a few days or a few weeks, followed by the pain of a breakup—until the next guy or girl comes along, and then the cycle begins again.

Neither type of serial dater is healthy in the long term. They have to deal with the possibility of sexually transmitted diseases or maybe just a bad reputation and hurt feelings. It's distressing to lose your heart to a person, who is not entirely there for you the way that you want to be for them. Many serial daters express they want to be with somebody permanently someday and will sometimes show that kind of commitment for a short time. Confusing and misinforming their companion, but in reality, they're not prepared and might never be. This is exactly what's known as unrequited passion. Whether you are the serial dater or the person they date, both experiences result in severe sadness and loneliness. It is better not dating than to date a serial dater or become one.

A <u>Perspicacious</u> Dater

A **perspicacious dater** [pur-spi-key-shuh s] has keen mental perception and an understanding that they are discerning. If there is no spark, perspicacious daters do not believe in wasting each other's time. They do understand no one is perfect on a first date, including themselves. If there is even a small spark, they will see where that leads. Sometimes it may just lead to having a new friend or an excellent relationship.

In the world of Internet dating, perspicacious daters realize people can be anything they want behind a computer screen. Sometimes people show potential in their profile, emails, or text messages, but when you meet them in person, there is no connection. If you know someone from church or maybe an exercise class, there is a chance you can formulate an opinion about him or her before the dating stage. Sometimes the more you get to know each other; you realize the less you have in common with this potential partner. Then some have initially presented themselves as totally different from their true selves.

Perspicacious daters realize dating is a filtering process, and they don't date just anyone. They are looking for the best partner for them and are not willing to settle for anyone just to have a partner. Sex is reserved for serious relationships, not random people. They are upfront and honest with all involved and never take advantage of anyone. Once they find someone with serious potential, they will date them and only them to see where the relationship goes. Perspicacious daters are happy with their lives.

I find perspicacious daters to be the most successful at understanding the essence of dating: an opportunity to make friends while finding out what you want in a relationship. They realize that dating and relationships are two different stages in the courting process. While dating, they do not have a physical relationship because that is best saved for when they are in a committed relationship. They understand dating is the time for learning about yourself, and having sex mixed in will not be fair to others you date. Most of all, you are doing yourself a disservice.

The Your Amazing Brain article "The Science of Love" shares how our brain entices us with an irresistible cocktail of chemicals during the three stages of love. Oxytocin and vasopressin are two hormones released during and after sex that do affect your brain to promote bonding and commitment. If you had an ex-partner who did not show you attention, and you rush into a new sexual relationship, you will be putting yourself at high risk of being hurt again or finding yourself in a relationship that is built around sex. Relationships that are built around only physical or financial factors will end in heartache or more loneliness than you had before.

When you decide to be exclusive and committed to one another, it is time to move to the next stage in courting, which is a relationship. Relationships come after dating because you are both aware of your goals for the future, what you want in a partner, and can fulfill each other's needs and desires. It is the time for building that strong foundation of the relationship that may lead you to the next stage, which is engagement, and then marriage. Just like when you were healing after your divorce, this chapter in your life is one step at a time.

> *It's one thing if you are just meeting different women for a drink or an occasional pizza, but once sex and deeper feelings enter the equation, you are starting to tiptoe through a very dangerous minefield.*
> —Matthew Fitzgerald, author and dating expert for *Ask Men* magazine

Why Men (or Women) Don't Approach You

This list was created to show the common mistakes people make at clubs. Unless you work at a club or bar, you will find only about 5 percent of the people who approach you will approach you at a club or bar; the other 95 percent will approach you everywhere else in your life. You will be surprised how many new people you meet if you recognize these factors that reduce your approachability:

1. *People of your same sex surround you:* This is the most common reason I have heard from men as to why they don't

approach women in bars or clubs. And most women tell me they are shy to go up to a group of men. Make sure to break away from the group every thirty minutes or so. Go to the restroom or go to the bar to order a drink alone. When you are doing "your solo" time, don't walk too fast; give potential partners a chance to approach in a natural fashion.

2. *People of the opposite sex surround you:* Men or women have no way of knowing what your relationship is with the people in your group. If you are with a group of people, make sure to distance yourself from the other men or women every thirty minutes or so and don't sit or stand next to just one of them. It gives others the impression you are with that person.

3. *You are wearing the wrong clothes:* Women tend to dress for the approval of other women. Don't look sloppy or too trendy because this seems to dumbfound men. When you wear clothes that are too sexy, you will probably be approached, but it will be for the wrong reasons. Men, make sure your clothes are clean and, if needed, ironed. Women do notice these things.

4. *You don't look happy:* If you tend to frown or make other faces that say, "I really don't want to be here," you are turning men or women away whether you know it or not. Smiling and eye contact is inviting, but looking like you're too good for everyone else has the opposite effect. Try to show a positive attitude, and more people will approach you.

5. *You are too busy:* We all have cell phones, and it's gotten to the point where we never have to be idle. A man or woman is not going to approach you if you are busy texting or buried in a book.
6. *You have a ring on your finger:* If you have any type of ring on your left hand—on any finger—a potential partner may view it as a sign that you are attached in some way. They will not take the time to see what type of ring it is.

We are in a new century; there is nothing wrong with smiling at someone and saying, "Hello." I have found this to be the best icebreaker and can lead to meeting someone. When you greet them with a smile, people view you as a friendly, kind, approachable person. A man or woman may give you their phone number when you least expect it.

The oddest meeting for me was when I had a car accident. On the back of the information card telling me where my car was being towed, the police officer wrote down his phone number and the words "I'm single." Most times just being the best that you can attract the opposite sex when you least expect it.

Rules for Dating?

Who came up with these so-called rules for dating? It must have been someone with a timeline to get you into bed. You need to understand from this day forward that you make your own rules! Let's look at the **Three-Date Rule**, which is a dating rule of thumb that states that the third date is when the decision is supposed to be made regarding whether a woman or man will consent to sex.

Like many longstanding traditions, it is difficult to trace the exact origin of this term. References are going back to the free love era of the late '60s and early '70s. I think that it is where this so-called rule and many others probably became popular. Having these rules promoted the free-love lifestyle. In case you didn't notice, we are in a new century, and it is time for a new rule. No one can tell you anymore what you should or should not do!

An anonymous poll carried out by **msn.match.com** among 5,237 singles of different ages suggests that in general there is no such rule, judging from the answers to the question: "How many dates does it take before you become intimate?"

- One: 12.74 percent
- Two: 24.94 percent
- Three: 21.48 percent
- Four or more: 34.18 percent
- Only after marriage: 6.66 percent

As you can see, many people set their own timetable for when they are willing to have sex. I have to say I was surprised to see almost 60 percent are having sex within the first three dates. I, for one, do not fall into that category.

When dating, you should do what is right for you. If you don't feel like kissing a person goodnight, then, by all means, don't. You do not owe anyone anything. When you agreed to go out on the date, it was merely an agreement to share time and your company with them and nothing more. Is there a price tag on a kiss? If so, then my price tag is really high. A hug, kiss, or sex is something that you offer when you are ready and comfortable; it is not up for sale. You are in control now, and no one can tell you what is right for you.

Here are my suggested dating rules: Throw out all the dating rules from the last century and make your own. I have only two rules. One is that I am honest about everything. I present myself as who I am, not who I think my date wants me to be. Second, I have no time limits on what I will or will not do because of the number of dates. I do what I feel is right, and I follow the Christian standards of my belief, and I conduct my life with the morals of my faith. I have to look myself in the mirror, and I judge myself regarding my actions. As humans, we all need and want sex. Don't do it before you are ready for any reason. When I find the right man and I am ready, he will be graced with a shared experience that he will never forget!

If Life Wasn't So Hard, We'd Value It Less

Because life is hard
And it causes a great
Deal of stress,
    Being human, it's
    Understandable
    That we get depressed.
If life wasn't hard, we would
Tend to value it a whole lot less.
    Common bonds are created
    Over issues that occur;
    Under siege we
    Learn to
    Defy the things we were,
Become that which we seek and
Exist as we prefer.
    We drop our guard,
    Obey our thirst, and drink at God's request,
    Rejoicing in the fact that we are blessed.
    So blessed to be the
    Evidence of what these words address ...
...And that is—If life wasn't so hard, We'd value it less.

                                                    —Tony Haynes

Chapter 4

Dating Safety

Date Smart and Safe, Not Fast and Reckless

Concerning dating, we all know safety is essential, but people have a tendency to share a significant amount of information regarding themselves as well as their children before they even go on the very first date. Doing this, you are not only putting yourself but also your family at an increased risk. My children are all adults; however, I still usually do not make references to my children by their names. Instead, I will refer to my daughter, my older or younger son, and possibly even use their nicknames, as I have done in the previous books in this series.

Drive yourself to the location of the date; you should not permit a stranger to know where your home is. Driving on your own is very convenient in the event the date is not going smoothly by doing, so it is now extremely easy for you to leave, knowing you will arrive home safely. While driving home, you should check your rearview mirror often and be aware of all vehicles to make sure you are not being followed. I have been followed after a date, but when I turned into the police station, for some strange reason, the driver of the other car decided to keep driving straight. Guess they didn't want to explain to the officer and me why they were following me when they lived on the opposite side of Houston.

Remember to exercise safety and caution in anything you do. I recommend individuals conduct background checks on just about every person they date, regardless of whether it is someone you knew in high school. You may very well not know what they have done since then; they may have been a guest of a state-run facility for an extended stay.

In my opinion, this is money very well spent. When people ask how I feel if a person does a background check on me, my response is that I expect that they should have; there is nothing in my background to cover up. Keep in mind that I do not share my last name or any private information about myself with a date until I am more comfortable with the individual. Then I am fine if they know where I live, along with other information regarding my personal life. You must achieve the safest dating experience possible.

In the event the person does develop into a potential mate, they will most likely be okay with respecting your privacy and permitting you the required time you need before revealing too much concerning your personal life.

> *Some people choose their company very carefully. A background check can help you feel more comfortable and secure when you branch out and meet someone new. Ultimately, you don't need to justify your reasons for performing a criminal background check. The information provided in most background checks is part of the public record. So, anyone can access background check data.*
> —Kat Saks of dmv.org.

Don't Trust in Others' Background Checks

Matchmaker services and some online dating sites do background checks on the people they take on as clients. That is one reason why most people pay the extra money for a matchmaking service. Keep in mind when dealing with matchmakers, though, that very often you still have to do your homework.

The matchmaker service my friend Helen was using would tell her a little bit about the person, and then she would look at the photos and descriptions of the person. Helen never found anyone who was appealing to her until one day; the matchmaker finally recommended a man named Drake. He and Helen went out on a date and had a lovely dinner, and initially, Drake seemed like a gentleman.

After a few dates, she decided to let him pick her up at her home because everything seemed to go very well. When Drake dropped her off one evening, he asked to come in and use the restroom, which seemed to take a long time. Helen found him walking around the house. When he saw Helen, he told her he had gotten lost.

When he returned, he asked Helen if she knew about the California love knot. Being the excellent sailor that she is, she decided it was time for the date to end. Histories of the love knot are linked to Celtic and Arabic cultures where young lovers used the knots to send secret messages to each other. The knot was thought to symbolize the inseparable joining of two hearts. The knots have been used in jewelry, crochet, and as a teaching tool for the basics of forming more complicated knots. Helen felt they had not been dating long enough to be talking about things like this. At that point, Drake turned into an octopus and was grabbing everything he could catch. Helen is a lady who is 5 foot 11 inches tall and grew up with four brothers, and since the door was fairly close, she was able to escape his hold reasonably quickly.

The next morning, Helen decided to do a background check on Drake herself. Much to her surprise, she got a lot of results back on this gentleman who was supposed to have a clear record. According to her background check, he had been arrested and convicted of burglary, assault, rape, and a few other charges. Helen was mortified that this man had been in her home. She started thinking about how long it took him to get to the bathroom and how he got lost on the way. Helen began to wonder if he was checking out the house to see if there was anything, he might be interested in appropriating for himself. Then she focused on his rape conviction and how he was such an octopus.

With all these concerns, she decided to call the matchmaker service and asked them why her background check showed all of these terrible things when theirs did not. They informed her that they knew about Drake's criminal record, but it was over seven years old, so they didn't report any of that information.

When you are dealing with rape, assault, burglary, and not just arrests but convictions that is vital information, I don't care if it happened over seven years ago; rape and assault frighten me.

Helen turned this company into the Better Business Bureau and posted a comment. She felt it was important to let people know that in her experience, this company was not interested in protecting its clients.

The bottom line is: If someone says they've done a background check on someone you're dating; you should still do one yourself.

Having Your Smart Phone Work for You

Once the person you are dating passes the email stage of getting to know you and you feel comfortable giving them your cellphone number, let your smartphone help you. Smartphones have many fields in the address book for listing information about your contacts. Here are a few things I do that have served me very well over time.

Start by putting the person's first name in the "first name" field. Then, in the "last name" field, type the last name if you have it, but if you don't, type in where you met the person and their username on the dating site (if it was online). If you later learn the last name, place it where it belongs and move where you met the person, et cetera under the organization, or work heading in the address book. Next, go to the site and take a photo of one of their photos, and assign one to their contact information. Having pictures of your contacts not only helps you recognize who is calling, but it can also help with texting, assisting you to make sure you are sending the text to the right person. I have sent a text to the wrong person on occasion.

In the notes area, fill in their birthday, children, what they do for a living, what part of town they live in, and any other information that you feel is important. It is also a great place to put notes from the things you discussed during your messaging phase. Fill in all other fields that you have information for, such as their email address.

I have also started using an app called YouMail. I use the free version, but if you don't have unlimited minutes, this is not for you. One of the features I like about the YouMail messaging app is that it allows the person calling to be greeted by their name. Other than just being a nice feature, this also has the positive effect of filtering undesirable dates. Someone that does not have good intentions may feel uncomfortable having the message call them by name.

If you decide you no longer want to talk to or text with a particular person, update their contact information, adding in all caps "DO NOT ANSWER" after the first name. The new contact information would look like this: "Ken DO NOT ANSWER Smith, Match.com, Ken1234."

If your address book has a send-to-voice-mail setting, turn that on. If you have YouMail, send the call to Ditch or block the call. If a ditched number calls you, the greeting can be set to tell the caller that your phone number is no longer in service.

Changing the name helps if they send you a text, so you will know not to respond. It is good to do even if you have a service like YouMail. There is nothing like thinking you're done with someone, and then a month or two later they call or text, and you answer by mistake, not knowing who they are because you have deleted their contact information from your address book.

Beware! Your Drink May Have a Date Rape Drug!

When I am out with friends, I often ask, "What would be a good topic for me to write about?" To my surprise, one night, I had three friends say at the same time, "Date rape drugs!" They all told me that within the last six months, all of them had been drugged. Years ago, the same thing also happened to me. Both sexes are at risk; I know of a few men who have been drugged. Here are some of the warning signs that you may have been the victim of a date rape drug, including what it feels like, what it does to you, and how you feel the next morning.

It only takes a second to put the powder or drops in a drink. In my case and the cases of two other friends, one male, and one female, we all believe the drugs were slipped in when our drinks were left unattended, either when we were dancing or talking to friends. Usually, date rapists rarely spend time with their victims before they slip the drug into their drinks; very often they slip the drug in before making contact with you. They will watch your drinking habits, then put the drug in your beverage or food at the right time so it will look like you have had too much to drink. After they have given you the drug, they wait and watch as it takes effect, and then they make their move to come and "help" you. I have just described the usual patters, though it was not the case with one of my friends. She found out that she was drugged when two male "friends" came up to her. While one hugged her, she turned her back on her drink, and the other put in the drops.

All of us had the same reaction to the drug. At first, we felt extremely dizzy. We experienced overwhelming fatigue. I felt like my whole body was just gone. Then, not understanding where we were or even caring about it, we had the feeling that everything around us was a dream or a movie, but the sound was not right. We were watching things with no feelings or emotions. We all also experienced difficulty walking, talking, and remembering things.

Even standing became almost impossible. The night is only a vague memory, and I am not sure what happened and what did not happen. The drug is usually out of your system in seventy-two hours, but some stay in longer. The most common date rape drug is GHB; it can be homemade and usually stays in your system for around forty-eight hours. The effects the drug has on your body usually last much longer. Because it knocks you out in a way that does not allow your brain to rest, all of us felt for days like we had a horrible hangover and the flu combined.

Sadly, none of the people who drugged us were ever brought to justice. We decided to list some of the mistakes we made to advise you on how you can avoid making them.

1. Remember that drinks in glasses are easier to put the drug in, so try to drink out of a bottle or a can that you open yourself.
2. Do not let anyone buy you a drink and bring it to you. If someone offers to buy you a drink, go to the bar with them and take it directly from the bartender. If a waitress is bringing it to you, take it from the waitress.
3. Make sure you include a nondrinking friend in the group, not only to drive everyone home but also to watch the drinks to make sure nothing happens.
4. Never turn your back on your drink, even to hug someone. Pick up your drink while you give a one-armed hug with your drink between you. Keep your drink in sight at all times.

5. Do not assume that because you are not drinking alcohol that you are safe. The person drugging you does not know what is in your drink.
6. If your drink tastes or smells strange, do not drink it. Usually, these drugs have no taste or odor, but since GHB is often homemade, you never know what they put into it.
7. Never leave your drink unattended, even for a second. If you left it unattended, pour that drink out and get another.
8. Do not share drinks or drink from a punch bowl. Any open container may already have the drug in it.
9. Just because a friend is supposed to be watching your drink does not mean they will keep a close enough eye on it. In many cases, the person who put the drug in the drink is frequently "friends" with the victim.
10. If you feel or felt drunk and did not drink alcohol, or you feel like the effects of alcohol are stronger than usual, get help immediately.

If you think you were raped, robbed, or drugged, go to a hospital immediately and let them know you suspect you were slipped some drug; they can test for them if they know to look. Blood can be tested up to twenty-four hours and urine up to ninety-six hours following ingestion.

For more information on date rape drugs, contact the following organizations that are listed below. If you live outside the U.S., please search on the internet to find some help close to where you are.

- **womenshealth.gov** at 800–994–9662 (TDD: 888 220–5446) or
- **Drug Enforcement Administration, DOJ Phone:** 202–307–1000
- **Food and Drug Administration, HHS Phone:** 800–332–4010 Hotline or 888–463–6332 (Consumer Information)
- **Men Can Stop Rape Phone:** 202–265–6530
- **National Center for Victims of Crime Phone:** 800–394–2255
- **National Institute on Drug Abuse, NIH, HHS Phone:** 800–662–4357 Hotline or 800–662–9832 (Spanish Language Hotline)
- **Office of National Drug Control Policy Phone:** 800–666–3332 (Information Clearinghouse)
- **Rape, Abuse, and Incest National Network Phone:** 800–656–4673

Dating after Divorce

The Courage to Care

*F*amiliarity with

*I*ndifference has made us immune to despair.

*N*o one gives a damn, not that a

*D*amn to give is fair.

I for one am insecure in this

*N*eo-soulless air.

*G*od, please help me find the courage to care.

*C*ommunity with

*O*pposition was served to leave my cupboards bare,

*U*ndermining a theme which gives

*R*edemption one more scare.

*A*nd still I dream of arrogance

*G*one with dinosaurs

*E*lsewhere …

… God, please help me find the courage to care.
We all mean well, and by all means
I long to do & dare.
God, please help me find the courage to care.

—Tony Haynes

Chapter 5

Online Dating

Dating Has Changed

Dating is not without its challenges. As someone who had a disfiguring accident in my twenties before my marriage, I have had difficulties in social situations at times. Even though, after three reconstructive surgeries, and had my lips tattooed with permeant lipstick to make the scar blend, most people don't see the scars, I still do, and meeting others has always been one of the most significant issues I have had when trying to date. A friend introduced me to online dating, and it changed my personal life as I knew it in a very positive way.

It had been over twenty years since I had been a member of the dating world. So much had changed, and I began to wonder if I was prepared to start my new adventure. There was no online dating before I got married, and like so many others, I relied on the church, friends, or other activities to meet potential significant others. Whether we like it or not, the Internet has changed our lives in many ways, especially how we meet and date people. Truthful people have the best shot at finding someone nice. Keep your expectations realistic, and don't be shy.

Social Networks and Online Dating

The distinction between social networks and online dating services is that online dating sites typically charge a fee, whereas social networks are complimentary. Many individuals are now choosing to make use of social networking services as an alternative to online dating sites. Some well-liked online dating services such as OkCupid.com, MatchMaker.com, Match.com, and eHarmony.com are seeing a reduction in members, whereas social networks like Plenty of Fish and Tinder (an app for cell phones) are experiencing a boost in users.

Dating online and meeting through social networks have become great ways to discover love and friendship. People are much more open to the concept of putting themselves out there on a dating site or social network—millions of people are on Facebook alone—and many more people join each day. As a result of this massive interest, paid dating sites and cost-free dating websites are improving their services with the use of more advanced technology to assist members in the search for a potential partner.

OkCupid.com has many questions that you can view the other person's answers. To see their response, you must answer the same question. I will admit some seem a little uncomfortable to answer. The website says this helps them match you better. I've noticed people with bad intentions usually either will not answer questions, or start messing up with their answers when you question something. The answers don't seem to match what they have said in their profile. The next advantage to OKCupids questions is with the uncomfortable questions. It is a useful tool that can either filter out the wrong person or take a second look at someone that has the same morals or desires.

Online dating can be enjoyable and safe as long as people use good sense and care when sharing their personal information. Most individuals who have experienced dating using a cost-free dating website or social networks have reported having the same results as they did on the paid dating sites. Everyone can share the same degree of success as long as you bear in mind that these services are just another venue to connect and meet others who are like-minded, and nothing more. You must additionally be safe and keep in mind that people may represent themselves in any way they prefer online, and they may not be as sincere as you are.

Online dating and social networks can be a less time-consuming way to meet new people from the surrounding area. Possibly the most fundamental advice when interacting with new people is generally to relax and be yourself. When beginning your communication with email, be personal and mindful of your safety. However, do not be too serious too soon.

It is essential to keep your sense of humor while online dating, just as it is equally vital offline. Online dating has many positive qualities if everyone is upfront about their expectations and honest about what they are bringing to the table.

Your Online Dating Profile Is an Advertisement about You

Writing an online profile is one of the most challenging things to do as you get back into the dating world. I have many pretty, smart, successful, funny friends who have accomplished many things in their lives, but writing a good online profile is just something they don't know how to do. One Saturday night, a group of friends were over, and one of them asked, "How do I make a good online dating profile?" I responded by telling them, "How about we go online and critique some profiles?" By the end of the evening, our tummy muscles had an incredible workout. Here are a few things we learned that evening from genuine online profiles.

Be as honest as you can, but please do not share all of your information. You may be an award-winning microbiologist, but that may scare more people away than it attracts. Many may think you are out of their league in the grey-matter category. So do not blow your own horn until they get to know how wonderful you are in so many other ways.

It is not wise to bring up certain things, like your grouchy teenagers or that your dog needs doggie diapers. Some people may think these things make their profile funny, but the reality is that many people do not take the time to read everything. People usually glance over profiles. If anything catches their attention, they will read that portion. Do you believe it is flattering to talk about your incontinent, Jack Russell? If a person does not look closely, and many don't, they may think you are the one with the problem, not Scooter.

Some people believe that mentioning sex should be part of your profile. I do not agree unless that is what you are looking for instead of a serious relationship. I would never tell a group of online strangers that I had not had sex in months. Sex does sell, but it sells to the wrong type of person, and those are not the ones I am trying to meet.

There is a lot to be said for keeping things simple, but not dull. Do not write a book when just a few, well-written paragraphs, would suffice. You need some things to talk about when you engage in further conversation through email, text, and chat, or for that first date.

Please don't make a checklist of things you want in a partner or about yourself. Here is a list of things we saw that you should not put on your profile—ever!

- "My biological clock is ticking, and I have the iPhone app that lets me know when I am ovulating."

- "I like poop and have unusual yet interesting bodily functions. Photos available."
- "I'm obsessed with my physique and will judge your every imperfection."
- "Oh, I am a crazy, crazy cat lady; where do I begin?"

Then there is the stuff we don't want to know because there must have been something in your past to make you write this

- "I don't like bondage, choking, or being hit or harmed in any way."
- "My children are adults, and I don't want to raise another."
- "If you are a jerk, just go to the next profile."

It is good, though, to bring up your deal breakers. People will then know where you stand on these issues and hopefully not contact you if they have a differing opinion.

This whole online profile thing is quite simple: Look at your profile as a little advertisement about you. You are competing in a market with all the other people doing the same type of ad. You want your ad to stand out as different from all the rest.

Most people scroll through all the photos included with a profile they are interested in to see if something sparks their attention. A current picture is a must for your profile. A current photo is a must for your profile. If you do not have a current photo, have one taken. Make sure the image reflects your personality, not what you believe your prospective date wants to see. If the picture is over two years old, be kind enough to disclose the year it was taken. Before posting, look at the entire background of your photo to check for tidiness and anything that may not need to be seen by a stranger. Many people do not realize the background of a picture tells others a lot about what type of person they are.

Your primary photo should be a headshot of yourself positioned correctly. Some friends may have said that pictures turned on their side to get more attention. Don't do that because many people now click past that person and go on to the next. Wear clothes in your photo; many people do not like to see lots of skin.

Types of photos to include in your profile:

- A headshot, as discussed above.
- One can show you at work, making sure to obscure any details regarding the name of the business or location. For example, if you are a businessperson, upload a photo that shows you dressed in business attire, or if you are a construction worker, including one of you wearing your hardhat.
- A picture of you doing something you enjoy, such as fishing or walking in the woods.

Your picture gallery can give the person information about who you are and what you like. Do not have a photo of yourself lying in bed or handing a drink to the camera unless that is the main reason for your online profile. Additionally, a photo of you dressed in an unusual costume is not a good profile picture unless it accurately depicts your personality.

When writing, be direct but include a little mystery. Flaunt what you've got modestly. Be brief, flirt a little, and be yourself. The first sentence must catch a prospective date's eye so that they will decide to read more. Try doing something a little different, something that will catch the proper type of person's attention. To give you an example, here is my current online profile.

> *"Romantic men seem to be extinct. If you're extinct, contact me."*
>
> *How many profiles have you read that start out saying how great the person is? I'm sure you have seen that frequently in all the other profiles of women trying to get your attention. I believe actions speak much louder, so why bother? I think I shall do something different and start with the bad stuff: I speak my mind, and I can be impulsive and restless at times. I have an eclectic taste in everything I do. Many days I spend too much time working; I need someone to take me away ... There is something about the water and being outside that I find magical. Can you relate? I have little patience for those who hide their emotions and will not speak their mind. I never know what they are thinking or planning. I prefer to know where I stand and what people think of me (good or bad), and I respect a person for letting me know. How about*

you? What irritated you today? Was there anything that gave you pure joy and pleasure?

It would be nice to meet a new friend and have coffee or some food at an outdoor restaurant. I don't think it matters what we do on our first meet and greet, as long as we have the time and opportunity to get to know one another. I am a big fan of simplicity, so a cup of coffee, tea, or hot chocolate would be excellent. Chemistry is something that you will know when you meet someone, not something you have with endless texts and e-mails.

Do you still enjoy laughing, smiling, or dancing in the rain? Do you still enjoy our beautiful, wonderful world and find it an interesting and exciting place to explore? Can you take a joke and understand that sarcasm is a spice of life? Can you enjoy a beautiful rainy day? If you are a self-motivated person and are generally happy. The rest is negotiable.

Thanks for stopping by and reading my profile, but I am not interested in a hook up of any kind, and I will only respond to men who are local, single (separated is not single), could not have attended the same school as my children, and who have a photo.

If you are a genuine, loving, caring, and fun person to be around, that doesn't sweat the small stuff in life; please message me.

I have had great success with this profile, and it weeds out many of the people who would not be compatible with me. Very often, when men contact me, they say they already felt like they knew me since I had given them lots of information about myself while still keeping all of my personal information personal.

Recently I saw one man's profile that caught my attention. His first sentence was, "I REALLY need a lady's point of view! In order to make my profile better, tell me what you find lacking or what was good about it." He is brilliant to ask women what they think. I am sure that sentence gets a lot of people to read his profile and probably respond to him. Yes, I responded to him and asked for him to give me a few pointers regarding my profile.

If you are stepping into the online dating world or you've been there for a while, take time to make your profile stand out from the crowd. Remember to use only current photos (two years or less) with you in them. An exception is a significant body change; in that case, use images after the major change occurred (such as a considerable weight gain or loss). Make sure to have one full-body shot. If you want to hold your tummy in for the picture, that is okay, but photoshopping to take off twenty pounds is not. Don't include photos without you in them just because they're beautiful. We all like to see a pretty sunset, but people are online to see you, not the sun setting. They can go outside and watch the sun go down for themselves. If you are an animal lover, it is fine to have photos of your pets. Just make sure you are in the photo with them.

Your success in online dating will start with how you complete your profile. Take time to make it as compelling and honest as you possibly can. Be kind toward yourself, yet accurate in all the information. Creating a fake profile or one that's too generous with the facts will make dating harder. With one look, your date will see you are shorter, years older, or heavier than you shared online. If you do find a person you appreciate being with, yet started with a false profile, the connection will probably end before the person has the chance to know the real you.

A few people have admitted to me that on a first date, they check the person out before they go to the table. One gentleman I know hid behind a potted plant for a few minutes to see how the woman related to people in the restaurant. If the date is different from the way they presented themselves online, these people told me they send a text stating they would not be able to make it for the date and then leave. The prevailing view is that if people lie about their appearance, they might lie about other things as well.

Keep your profile short, only a few paragraphs long, making sure to ask a question or two that will show what kind of person you are. It will give potential dates something to say when sending you a message. Be yourself, and if the profile doesn't work for you, try rewriting it again and again.

Netiquette

Just as there is etiquette when dating, there is netiquette with online dating. You cannot have one rule for yourself and another for your date and then expect everything to be okay. When dating online, please keep these things in mind, and your experience will go much better.

- Do not respond with one-word replies; instead, you should use complete sentences, so there is no ambiguity with your response. Try to communicate with your online date as you would if you were sitting down talking with a friend.
- Do not use all capital letters because this means you are "SHOUTING." Yes, Yes, I know I did just used all caps in the words really and shouting. I wanted to stress the point, but I did not write the entire sections in capital letters.
- Do not only talk about yourself; ask them questions, since the conversation is a two-way form of communication. Start with things they have put in their profile, for example, their likes and dislikes, hobbies, and so forth.
- Use your spell check and then re-read the message before you send it. Occasional errors are fine, but you don't want to appear deficient in the grey matter by making error after error.
- Be polite: no swearing or saying anything that would be hurtful to the other person. Also, don't ask any rude questions. Avoid topics that might be considered racist or obscene.

- If you have to end the conversation, tell them so, and send a short note thanking him or her for their time. That way, they also will know the conversation is over.

- Do not give them a full history about yourself in the first two communications. Take your time and enjoy learning more about this person. It will help to establish a comfortable feeling as you start to learn and share.

- If you feel that someone is harassing you or being abusive, then you should promptly cut off the conversation. Additionally, report them to the dating site and the police if necessary.

- Do not talk about marriage or marriage proposals. If you think people have not done this before, give me a call, I have some stories to tell that will make you shake your head in disbelief.

- Do not send any photos of yourself that you would not share with children. I am sure I do not need to elaborate on what type of photos those are. Two men I know admit they have sent a picture or two of their private parts to someone they had just met online. All I can say is, think first. If in doubt, don't hit send. Anything you send can be forwarded all over the Internet. While we are talking about photos, keep your children out of the picture, and if you are using your cell phone, keep the GPS off when taking the photo, so no location is saved with the photo data.

Setting Up an Email Account to Use with People You Meet Online

Many people do not notice that your personal information will show up when you communicate with instant messaging (IM) or emails. They assume that the only information available is your email address. Unfortunately, this is not the case. Go into your emails and look all over the page, not just at the email message's contents. Many have the sender's personal information, including a photo. Without realizing it, if you click on the IM, you will see the person talking to you has private information about you. In addition to putting yourself in physical danger, they could also steal your identity. That is why many people you meet online will ask you to IM them on Yahoo, or Google.

There are steps you need to take to prevent this, and they are almost effortless to execute. First, set up a new email account exclusively for online dating. I have used Google, and below, you will see the steps I took to set up a safer email account.

- Click "Create an Account" on the main page. Your first name should be something you make up, such as part of your dating username (like "Lady In"). Your last name should also be something you make up, in this case, the other part of the online username ("Town").

- Now create your email address. If it is available, use your dating username@whatever.com. In this example, it would be ladyintown@gmail.com.
- Your password should be a mixture of letters (upper- and lowercase) and numbers. The use of passphrases for complexity is more important than password length. Even add symbols if you like.
- Do not use your real birthday; make sure your fake age is over eighteen years old.
- There are many areas you don't even have to fill out. Rule of thumb: Do not fill out anything you don't have to. Here are two fields you must leave blank: your current email address and your phone number. Giving this information will link this new account to your main account and give out information you are trying to protect. This email account must be a standalone account and not connected to anything else.

Emailing is an excellent way to find out a bit more about each other to see if you click. Protect any personal information, making sure not to include it in the emails you send. If you are referring to your children, write "my daughter" or "my son"—not their real names. When referring to where you live, don't reveal your neighborhood or any information someone can trace back to your actual location. These tips are designed to protect you from those who are just trying to take advantage of you. Make sure you are still cautious until you know a person is genuine.

The Process for Dating Online

Browse around and flip through many profiles: The first step is to look through the profiles. Using an advanced search will help you to narrow down the search process and find someone compatible with you. Make sure to read the profiles carefully so you can find someone you would like to get to know better. Don't just look at the pictures. Hopefully, they are as honest as you and also have a current photo, but I have found that this is not always the case. Look at many profiles and find a few that you are attracted to, but not just in the sense of physical looks. Look for a profile that you feel you mesh well with, someone with values and lifestyle wishes that are similar to your own. You can tell a lot about a person through their profile, so you should pay careful attention when browsing to look for a new mate.

Look closely at the photos: If the person does not have a main profile photo that shows what they look like, skip to the next profile. There is probably an excellent reason they don't have a photo or have a picture of something other than themselves. Other problematic main profile photos are group shots, blurry images, or those where they are so far away; it is difficult to see how they look. These types of profile photos are attempts to hide their identity, and you should avoid the person at all costs. Don't fall for they will privately email you a better picture. If they have a better one, why isn't it on the dating site already?

Make sure to zoom in and see what the background looks like in all the photos on the profile. Stop looking at the person for a moment and check out everything else the photo can share with you. I have seen two recent photos that had interesting details. One was of a gentleman in his living room; on the wall behind him was his wedding photo. The other was a neonatal doctor holding the hand of one of his patients. His left hand had been cropped, but not enough to take off the corner of the ring finger, which had a gold band on it. I don't know many divorced men who still display their wedding photos or wear a wedding ring.

Is it possible a person could use a photo taken before they were divorced? If that is the case, they will have no problem explaining the picture, and you both will have a good laugh about it. However, if you don't hear from them again, they get angry, or you look at their profile and the photo has been removed or cropped, then they probably should not have been on the dating website.

Thanks, but no thanks: If someone shows interest in you by sending a wink, liking one of your photos, or sending an email, and you know there is no spark at all, be kind and send an email back to them stating something like, "Thanks for contacting me, but I don't feel we are a good match at this time. Good luck in your search." By doing so, you are not leaving them hanging, wondering if you are interested. It is a polite thing to do and always friendly to thank them for their interest. Keep in mind that just because you're online does not mean you are not expected to treat people with proper manners.

Send an excellent email introduction: As you have always heard, first impressions are crucial. Your first email introduction should state a little bit about you and a bit of what you liked about the person's profile. When you send an email, to get an almost guaranteed response, ask the other person a question. Not only are questions often replied to, but also expressing some interest in the person, and their life or thoughts will make you look more appealing. Remember to send emails to different prospects during the first phase of dating. You need to offer yourself some variety and increase the chances of finding someone interesting. Only yakking about yourself is not a good idea. What is there to say to that? I recommend starting with just a quick note. Keep it simple at the beginning; just be yourself. At this stage, you should use the online dating service's email, not your private email.

Follow up: If you sent an introductory email, and they do not respond within a week, it is okay to send one follow-up. It will show the person you are interested in them. If they do not respond to the second email, they are probably not interested. Some sites give you the ability to block people from seeing your profile, so use it if it's available. Doing this will also remove the person from showing up as a suggested match for you. Keep in mind that some people go off the site for a few months and then come back on. Before you block someone, check to see the last time they were on the site. If they are not a paying member, it's possible they can't respond; most places that charge for their services will not allow people to receive or send emails if they are not paying members.

In many cases, the follow-up email will start a new conversation. Life can and does get busy at times. The person may have gotten busy after reading your email, meant to respond, then forgot when things slowed down."

Take a screenshot of their profile with your cell phone. On most cell phones if you press the power and home button together, you will have a screenshot that will go into your photos. While you're at it do a screenshot of the entire profile. Then you will have it at easy access to refer back to when you are communicating without having to go back and look at their profile repeatedly.

Giving them your private email or using an app like kik offers a private means of communication: When you have communicated for a while, and both of you would like to have a more open line of communication, here are a couple of options you might want to consider. Kik is a wonderful app to communicate that is way more than just messaging and sharing pictures. It does not require you to use or expose your phone number. All you have to do is pick a username. While setting up your account, remember you do not have to fill out all your personal information, so take advantage of that benefit. Another option is to use an email account that you have set up just for dating. This one should have no personal information about you and should not be connected to any of your other email accounts. Some favorite email clients are Yahoo and Google, which have instant messenger (IM) capabilities, as discussed above. For a while, keep all of your personal information protected. It is okay to give matches your first name at the beginning of this process, but hold off on divulging your last name for the time being.

Exchanging phone numbers: After you feel more comfortable, you can move on to phone communication. If you can afford it, consider getting a disposable cell phone. Some dating sites offer a phone service for an extra fee, and you might want to consider this option. Landline numbers are easy to trace, and people can get all kinds of information, including your home address. With cellphones, it is a little bit harder to obtain personal information than from a landline. There are people who email and text wonderfully, but when you talk to them on the phone, you see there is no connection or attraction to the person. So, don't skip the phone chat before arranging a meeting.

Take your time: Occasionally, wait for at least two to four hours before replying to an email or text. You want to appear active, confident, and involved in life, even if you are sitting home in your pajamas, watching TV. That may be what you're doing, but they don't have to know that. Remember, part of dating attraction is the chase. If it appears you have a fulfilling, busy life and others are interested in you, often people will be more attracted to you.

Do a Google search, Spokeo.com search, Truthfinder or any similar background check: By now you should have your match's first and last name, along with their age. You can download their online dating profile photo to Google Image search, and it may reveal information about the person. For a basic background or Google search, this is all the information you need. While doing your search, keep in mind information on the internet searches are only as good as the information that was put in. An occasional error will pop up on your internet searches at times. There is no need to do a full-blown, how-many-hairs-they-have-on-their-head background check because you do want to have things you can learn about your date. But it is imperative to verify that they are not married and if they have or have not been a guest of the state for an extended period of time.

We are living in a new cyber age, so remember people can present themselves very differently from who they are and hide whatever history they may not want you to know. I am okay with anyone doing a background check on me, and I feel if anyone has a problem with me running a background check on them, then they probably have something to hide.

Viber, IMO, Skype or FaceTime: Have a date in the safety of your own home while your match is in the safety of their home. Being careful about what is in the background where you are sitting is very important. Before your video date, make sure to check and look closely at everything the camera is picking up behind you. Making sure it is not revealing more information than you are ready to share with your prospective date. Based on what your test run revealed adjust your background accordingly

The apps IMO, WhatsApp, and Viber let you message and video chat for free, no matter what device they are on. Make free video and voice calls over your Wi-Fi connection as long as you both have the same app on your phones.

Set up a specific time for a video date, possibly over coffee. Both of you could even have dinner prepared and enjoy a meal together via cyberspace. Remember just because you have skyped or video chatted does not verify anything other than the appearance matches the photos.

Meet and greet: Before you agree to a date that could last hours, it is best to meet in a very public place for a cup of coffee, ice cream, or something else that could give you the opportunity for a short introduction to each other. The two of you are meeting to see if the chemistry that was there online is there in person.

It is okay if you're not physically attracted to each other; you may have just made a new friend. You never know—that friendship could lead to you finding the love of your life. The meet and greet will give you enough information to see if you want to attempt to build something with this person and continue to date, or if you want to leap back into the dating pool with a splashing cannonball. If you are attracted and they haven't broken any of your deal-breakers, set up a date.

First date: Congratulations! You have made it to the first date. Now see where this first date leads. It is best to find an activity to do where you will not feel obligated to stay, and no one will have hurt feelings if either of you decides to cut the date short.

Just as with your meet and greet, make sure you go to a public place where you can talk and get to know one another. Since talking during a movie is not polite to others, going to see a movie is not advisable for a first date. Good choices for a first date are the zoo, a museum, or somewhere else the two of you could chat. One of my friends has a zoo membership and is allowed to take a guest whenever he goes. Cal has taken this idea a step further to show the woman he notices the little things. During the emails, texts, phone calls, and meet and greet, he finds out some of the unique little things the woman he is interested in enjoys eating and drinking. Before going to the zoo, Cal places many of the items she has mentioned in his backpack. While they stroll through the zoo, he offers her some of the tasty treats she has said she enjoys.

The old saying goes, "You have to kiss a lot of frogs to find your prince or princess." With online dating, you're not kissing, but you are communicating, so if at first, you don't succeed, try, try again. You may have to go through a few frogs to find your prince or princess. In my case, there have been more frogs than anything else, but luckily enough, I'm not squeamish. The important thing is getting back onto the lily pad and giving online dating a try. The pond is much larger, and princes and princesses abound!

What are the Odds? Safety Is an Issue for Both Sexes

My friend Art, like many of us, had been in a long-term relationship that ended, and he started online dating. Like most men, he thought things like safety were only issues women needed to be concerned with and take the proper precautions. He felt he was a man and could take care of himself, but did the basics to protect his identity because he didn't want my redhead Irish/Scottish attitude unleashed upon him.

He met a nice woman online, and they seemed to have everything in common. They talked on the phone and decided to meet for a date. About fifteen minutes after their date was supposed to begin, Crystal texted that she was running late and asked Art to wait for her at the bar instead of getting a table. While Art was waiting at the bar, a man came up and struck up a conversation with him. He said he was also there are for a first date with someone he'd met online. The man was nice enough, but Art noticed he just seemed a little out of place for the restaurant. Then Crystal called and told him she was sorry she couldn't make it, and she would like to reschedule another date. The next day, I called to ask about his date, and Art gave me a few details. I told him what happened didn't sound right. I asked, "What are the odds that both of you are meeting an online date at the same time and place, but neither date shows up?" I stressed to him that when they rescheduled the date, they should go to my favorite Midtown restaurant that has my favorite staff.

The next date was set. Once again, Crystal called and said she was running late and would he, please wait at the bar for her. When Art walked into the bar, he was a little surprised to see the same gentleman sitting in the bar. The man motioned for Art to come over and suggested they once again wait together. My words "what are the odds" kept ringing in Art's ear. So he looked a little more closely at the man and noticed a few prison tattoos.

Robert, my favorite waiter, was walking by, and Art said, "Hey Robert, T told me you were from the Midwest." That's one of my code phrases for "I need to get out of here." Without missing a beat, Robert said, "Sure am, and by the way, the hostess has a question about your reservation." Art headed straight toward the hostess. He handed her a twenty for his drink. He told her to tell Robert thanks and to keep the change.

The next day, Crystal went into overdrive, sending numerous texts, emails, and calls pleading for another date. After reflecting on all the information Art had given Crystal, he felt sure the only thing she had of his personal information was his cell phone number. That afternoon he decided to use his YouMail app on his cell phone and put her in the "ditched" category.

About a month later, Art was watching the news and saw that the man from the bar and Crystal, they were arrested for aggravated robbery. The report also stated additional charges were pending because the police did not know if the man would survive the brutal attack, he had gotten in the restaurant's parking lot. Art was initially upset that on his date nights there was no parking and he'd had to use the valet, but now he was very thankful. Right after the news aired, he said a little prayer thanking God for the lack of parking spaces.

Prison Tattoos

Art and I are very fortunate to have a friend who is a deputy in the sheriff's department and works at a jail in Texas. When I started in my new dating life, Mark stressed safety. One afternoon he sat me down and gave me a crash course on what to look for if I see someone with a tattoo. Prison tattoos represent a controversial subculture in the tattoo community. Often, they are crude in technique, but as Mark believes, there may be no style of tattoo that is as full of symbolism and meaning. Mark will identify gang members by their tattoos and segregate them from other prisoners to prevent fights from breaking out in the jail.

Getting tattoos while serving time in the penitentiary has always been a big part of prison culture. Today prison tattoos are usually used by inmates to identify themselves by their name or prison ID. Offenders get tattoos for a variety of reasons. Some choose to be tattooed as a way of expressing racial pride or gang affiliation, while others do it as a way of repelling bullies or sexual predators.

Some prefer to do an old-school way with pure ink and a needle. Now many prison tattoos are done with the use of a motor and pen ink in a sort of makeshift prison tattoo machine. The ink is usually one color, either black or blue. It may turn to purple depending sun exposure and the skin's pigment. Most often, but not always, these tattoos are a bit crude, sloppy, and very noticeable—nothing like the quality or colors you see at a tattoo parlor.

Let's talk about the three things the ink tells you. First of all, it may determine who the person is and possibly a loved one's name. Second, it shows what they have done, and it may relate to their crimes. For example, if they have a gun tattoo and it is pictured from the side, this means they carry a gun. If the weapon is pointed outward, this means they are a shooter. Lastly, the tattoo shows what prisons they have called home. Very often these will be landmarks, sometimes even including walls, gun towers, cell doors, or windows. Remember to take your time and read the ink like a book. From left to right and from top to bottom, look at tattoos carefully: there are stories within stories.

If you think your date has a prison tattoo, and they have never told you they were in jail, I would advise you to slow things down and do a background check before you even think about seeing them again. If you are like me, this may be something you never thought you needed to know about, but now that you are in the dating world, you need to be able to recognize things that people may be withholding from you. We all have baggage from our past, but if someone has served time in prison, and withheld that information, that would be something I would be afraid of seeing the person any further.

For more information, check out prison tattooing on Wikipedia.

Safety Tips for Online Dating

The Internet is still pretty safe, even for seniors, according to WiredSafety.org. People are emailing, private messaging, chatting with one another, and making cyber-dates. Online dating can be a fun and fulfilling experience, as long as you stay safe. In addition to the safety measures already mentioned, here are a few additional precautions to ensure your safety and success.

- **Make sure your computer is secure:** Are your computer's anti-virus program and firewall all up to date? Is your wireless network secure? Do you have strong passwords that contain a mixture of letters and numbers? I also use an identity protection program and recommend them. Don't let identity thieves ruin your life.

- **Be wary:** Do not believe everything you read online. The person on the other computer could be a child or someone faking their gender.

- **Keep copies:** If something goes wrong, you need to have copies of your communications in a file so that you can show friends or the police if you need to. I also have a recovery app that sends a copy of all my texts to my email account (another a good idea for communicating with your ex; for more on that topic, please see the first book in this series, *Divorced and Scared No More: Emotional Support for the Newly Divorced*).

- **Watch in your rearview mirror on your way home:** If you think you are being followed, go to the nearest police station. I am sure the person following you won't want to follow you in there and have to explain why they were following you.

An excellent place to find more information regarding Internet safety is WiredSafety.com

A Date May Be Different from How They Present Themselves Online

Many times, when filling out an online profile, people stretch the truth, and Bridget was an expert. Rodney had been communicating with Bridget for about a month, and they finally decided to meet and go out for dinner date. When Rodney got to the restaurant, he noticed Bridget's weight was more like 195 pounds, not 110 pounds. That was just the beginning of the "exciting" differences from her profile. As they were eating, she mentioned her twenty-four-year-old son. A few moments later, Rodney was reminded that she said she was thirty-five. Was she eleven years old when she had her son? As dinner progressed, Rodney started noticing that every time one of her falsehoods came out, Bridget's fork shook like it was a little lie detector. When the topic got around to previous marriages, he realized she had been married eight times. Bridget hadn't counted one marriage because she had it annulled, but her online profile stated that she had been married twice. She also seemed to be a little frustrated about the one that was annulled all these years later. Her husband left her for another man, and her family sided with him.

Rodney decided there was just too much information that Bridget had stretched, and this was probably the tip of the iceberg. After dinner, he politely walked her to her car, thinking he only had a few more minutes with Bridget. As he got closer to the vehicle, he noticed she had a flat tire. The gentleman that is he is, Rodney could not just turn around and walk away. He started changing the tire, and of course, Bridget didn't offer to help. She did keep questioning if he was doing it right.

Then it started to rain. Bridget walked to the car and got in with no concern that Rodney was in the process of changing *her* tire. While getting in, Bridget commented that she did not want to get wet or mess up her hair. After about five minutes, she started tapping on the window. Rodney looked up and saw that she looked quite irritated. She rolled down the window and said, "Can you hurry up? I'm running late." Rodney felt like saying, "Lady, finish it yourself," but he is such a southern gentleman that he finished changing her tire. A few days later, Bridget texted him and asked when they would be going out again. Rodney sent her a text back, explaining he felt they were not a good match and wished her well in her search. Even though you have filtered online profiles and you have done your texting, emailing, and completed a background check, often you will find that your date still may not be quite the way they presented themselves online. But don't fret just because you come across a bad date or two; we have all had them. In the world of dating, think of it as a stop along the journey to find that perfect mate who will still be next to you when you both reach your destination in life.

Is Someone Trying to Catfish Me or Is This Person Real?

Sometimes the person you read about on an online dating site is not the same person typing in the information. When someone is catfishing, they pretend to be someone they are not by using the Internet to create false identities, and their primary goal is to pursue deceptive online romances. The person behind the profile may be married, a person of the opposite sex than you are interested in, a young person, or someone out to do you harm. There are stalkers online, and some people are out to steal your identity. There are many people from other countries who are trying to get into the country you live within. They may be targeting you as their ticket into the land of their dreams. Many are successful, but usually, there are red flags.

Some of these people will send you a standard, generic email they send to everyone the first time they contact them. Some are a little smarter and put a few comments about your profile in their message, and then there are a few who do read your profile and emails, then ask you questions. Most of the emails will have many compliments about how wonderful you look or how you have a great smile. Typically, they love your profile but give no details as to why. These writers also usually claim to be financially secure and have a successful job. They tell a sad story about why they are on the

Internet, looking for a soul mate. They usually want you to get off of the dating site's email service and onto instant messaging quickly. Let's take a look at emails I received from a man named "Daniel." See if you can find the red flags. I have used asterisks (*) in place of the last name, dating site name, and the company name he gave. The emails are just copied and pasted so you can learn from them.

Hi its Daniel ******, from the ***** dating site. im getting a spark towards you already,

Well a little about me..im a 51 years old single Man from California , but spent most of my life in Texas , I have a master degree in Business Administration from University of Hull in 1988.. I'm an Operational Manager for ***** Oil. Would be leaving for England in a few days to secure a contract. I am online looking to build a relationship with someone special, So When we meet, we wont be like strangers to each other. I have a 26 years old Son., Hes name is Emric and he lives in Canada. His mom passed away shortly after our divorce. What about you.? why are you on here?

I'm Divorced, My Ex wife cheated on me with my friend, I was really hurt and gave my self a long time alone because i became scared of women, But right now i'm ready to love again.. Im now in search of my soul mate, someone i can settle with as soon as i get back home. i'm ready to relocate anywhere she is. What are you looking for? From you profile, I see you are looking for the something similar, Hope you are ready to trust and be honest? Am ready to give all.

Also i'm a clean type of guy. i love to cook, watch sports,play pool, bowl,workout,go out to dinner and movies,read investment magazines also..

Im intelligent, loving, caring, honest, caring, understanding,romantic and respectful, Im the type of guy you can bring home to your mom..lol Would love to chat on yahoo messenger, It easier and faster on there sweetie look forward to reading from you

xxx

This man says he graduated from the University of Hull and is an operational manager—but look at the grammar, spelling errors, and the use of capital letters. He also says that from my profile, I am looking for something similar. As you saw in my profile, I never mentioned anything related to his comments or anything in his profile. And, of course, we have his suggestion that we talk on Yahoo instant messenger.

After I received this email, his profile was taken off the dating site. Messaging with him was still available on the site. Here are three reasons why a profile could be removed: the person removes it, the person was reported to the online dating service, or the person blocks you from seeing the profile. In a message, I expressed my concern that his profile was no longer on the online dating service, and this is the email I got in response:

Thanks again for getting back to me..I do really Appreciate it, I would be leaving tomorrow. Well i want you to know that this is my first time doing this online stuff, A very good friend of mine introduced me to this internet dating, he found his soul mate on here and i thought i would give this a try as well...so tell me how long you have been doing this online internet dating and how many people have you met on the internet,? You are the first person i'm trying this with and i hope that it does work out for me(us). My job is quite hectic but very rewarding .

More also, A Little more about me,I like to do all the normal things that a human loves doing. I want to find my best friend and lover wrapped up into one. I guess best friend and lover wrapped up into one really doesn't describe it the way I would like.I want to meet that life partner that I can not wait to wake up in the morning to see or get home from work to share smiles, laughs and good conversation. I want to be able to pick up the phone at work and tell that special somebody what the goofy person in the next office over just did. I would like to meet that one person the person that will love me as much as I love will love her,And also show each other the love in little special ways,I am sick and tired of games!!!!. Send lovely E cards for no reasons or cook some soup when you are feeling under the weather. I guess you get the hint. I am a romantic and I do believe that my one love

> is out there...I would be looking forward to read from you and if you are really serious about getting to know one another even with the Distance then write back. Im willing to build a connection so when we meet we wont be like strangers. Tell me why you are concerned cause i took my profile out.
>
> Dying to read from you again. Love

Do you notice the same grammar and spelling errors in this message from a supposedly very educated and successful man? The interesting point to see is he does not answer my question as to why the profile is gone, but he ends the email with "Love." I sent another email asking why his profile was off the online dating service, and this is what I received back.

> Hello Pretty
>
> Nice to read from you, i totally agree with you and i have attached a photo of me,i want friend at first and would also love to see where it leads .
>
> Here is a few question i have for you, i really understand all what you have said
>
> What do you do for a living?
> What do you seek for in a relationship?
> What sort of relationship you seek for?
> What are the basic qualities you seek for in a Man?
> What do you do for fun?
> Do you like public intimacy?

> . *How do you treat your Ideal man?*
> *Tell me Why you need a Man?*
> *Can you love this Man?*
> *Would you hit your Man for any reasons?*
> *Hope you had a nice time this weekend, i really look forward to reading your letters soonest. did you get the yahoo messenger?*
> *xx*

I think this person was trying to catfish me and was probably from outside the country trying to get in. My emails back to him only asked why his profile was off the dating site and nothing more. In his emails, why did he "agree," and what did he agree with? Why didn't he answer my question?

Here is an example of another message from a person who also was a potential catfisher.

> *Hi .*
>
> *Am using this medium to inform you that my story was a success via ***** online dating as i found my partner and we are getting married in two weeks time from now. I was online today, about closing my ***** account since i already got a life partner when My Australian Friend Donovan who isn't into internet dating came across your profile through my ***** account as he was actually standing behind me and he's been all over me about getting in touch with you, he said you seem like a woman whom has*

found balance in all aspect of Life which is a hard thing to come by these days and also the smile you put on caught his attention. He's 6'2' tall, 55years old, Widower, a good Listener,very good Looking and all rounded a complete Guy with a good proffesion in US Army ,I didn't tell him I was gonna contact you, but thought I take a chance, you never know until you try, it might worth it in the end. take a chance and e-mail him, he'll share a picture and more information with you,

his direct e-mail addy is *******01 / at / yahoo /dot/ com . hope you can decode that lol, as ***** will not allow me send the e-mail directly.

Sorry to bother you, one thing I can assure you is you'll brighten his day if you do get in touch with him. Am closing my account now with this little hint and i believe if my story can be successful, yours too will be.

Have a wonderful day...

Since this message was from a woman who lived out of state, my settings sent it to the filtered mail folder. I did not see it until eleven days after it was sent to me. I decided to click on her profile to see if she had deleted her account, and I found it was still active. She had used it within the last twenty-four hours. Although the profile itself did not have any red flags and she seemed pretty reasonable, the simple fact that she still had the account and it was being used was a problem. If her friend was accessing the online dating site though her account and wanted the people, he contacted to go directly off the safety of the dating site, that's a red flag because he had not set up his profile, thus hiding his identity.

I hope you see the pattern in these emails; they complimented me excessively and tried to convince me to communicate off the dating site quickly. These are just a couple of examples of things to look out for when you are online. If you get any messages like this, do not respond. I only responded to "Daniel's" messages so I could get emails for you to learn from and what should send you a red flag or two. A question I pose during the messaging phase to weed out some of these people is "I live in ____ on the ____ side what part of town are you in?"

Are They Hiding Something?

Voucher Codes Pro recently conducted a survey in the UK and found that 58 percent of online daters had lied about themselves to impress a prospective partner. In the study, men lied most about their employment, age, and marital status, while women tended to lie more about their weight or body shape. We are all imperfect, but being authentic and genuine is very important in finding a new partner.

While it is not possible to eliminate every possibility of encountering people who misrepresent themselves on the Internet, there are several ways to determine if someone is likely to be different from who they have presented themselves as (such as being married when they claim to be single).

Learn these possible signs that someone may be misrepresenting themselves:

- **Photos that hide something:** Putting up a photograph from a great distance, a blurry photo, an old photo (such as a childhood snapshot or old school picture), a photo that doesn't show the face (a back or side shot), a group photo, only one photo, a photo of an object (such as a sunset or dog), or no primary photograph at all are all tactics of people trying to conceal their identities. If they are using a group photo and their partner finds out the picture is on the site, they will use the excuse that it was a friend's account and they just happened to be in the photo. If you have to ask which person they are in the picture or request one, they are probably hiding their identity for a reason.
- **Details that don't seem right:** Look for further information on the photos, such as wedding rings and pictures on the walls that may contradict how they have presented themselves.
- **Déjà vu:** If the profile looks familiar, it may be because many of these people will cut and paste others' profiles.
- **Restrictions on communicating with you:** If the calls you make to them go straight to voicemail, or if their responses to your emails and text messages are irregular and erratic, they are probably juggling a family life along with their online dating life.
- **Secretive behavior:** While it is normal for people to hold back initially if they have something to hide, they will usually not

reveal details about where they live, their work, their family, upbringing, and so on. They don't want you to have too much information so you can't do an Internet search on them.

- **Fear of background checks or Internet searches:** Recently, one police officer who I was considering dating burst out laughing when I mentioned that I do background checks and recommend others do them as well. Then he said, "That's fine, I already did one on you. People with nothing to hide have no problem with it. If they get upset, then you usually already have your answer before the background check is done."

Be prepared; some bad people will try to give you falsehoods to cover up what they know will show up on a background check. For example, one man told me he had worked undercover for the government. Therefore, he would have a few things show up, but the charges were dismissed because he had to get arrested and charged so he could stay undercover. I didn't just glance over those charges like many people may have done. Instead, I read the details. When I asked Gill why he was convicted of a few of the serious charges and let him know I knew what his penalties for them were. At that point, he did not deny anything and told me the background check was correct.

- **Minimal information in their profile about themselves:** If they are leaving most things blank and asking you to ask them about themselves, then you are probably not going to be getting accurate information. They may give the responses they think you would like to hear.

- **Plans to move:** If they live out of town or out of state and they say they are preparing for a move to your area, or they claim to come to your area on business frequently, so your space is like a second home to them, be wary.

- **A pattern of contact:** If they have a pattern regarding when they are online, calling or texting you only at certain times of day, this is because they don't want their partners to know they are talking to an online date.

- **Talking in hushed tones or hanging up abruptly:** If this happens, it is almost certain the person is hiding something.

- **Hiding their address:** If you have started dating and the person refuses to share their address with you, even though they know your address and have been to your home, that's a sign the person is hiding something.

- **Different private and public behavior:** Does this sound familiar? In public, the two of you are like acquaintances on a joint outing, and they keep looking at the door or over their shoulder. In private, behind closed doors, or in a car, they become very affectionate.

Things you can do:
- Avoid people with profiles or issues similar to the ones listed above. It is best not to engage because more than likely, you are setting yourself up for a complicated situation.

- Just as you should periodically do Google searches (including an image search) for your name, conduct background checks on yourself to protect your identity.
- Consider using a paid online dating site. Married people are less likely to use paid sites because they do not want the credit charge to show up on their statement.
- Ask them to take a photo holding something specific, such as a piece of paper with a particular phrase written on it. If someone asks you for this, do not hold up your driver's license. Remember, people can zoom in on these photos to find personal information about you.
- Have a virtual first date using Viber, IMO, WhatsApp, Skype, or FaceTime. Most of today's smartphones, tablets, and laptops come equipped with the technology for video chatting, or you can get an app. If they are reluctant to speak on live video, claiming shyness or that they can't find a camera, that's usually a sign that this is a person to avoid.
- If they are not available to you when you call, text, and email, or have a pattern regarding contact with you; then you must ask them why.
- When you share your address with someone, find out their address as well.
- Ask to meet their friends or have a few of them over to your house for a cookout one weekend.

Some people are simply shy or cautious when they date. Perhaps they are dating multiple people but feel they need to hide the fact. Or maybe they are just not sure if they are interested in you, and they're holding back. Only because people like this exist doesn't mean you should ignore the warning signs. If, when you ask for some of the things I suggested, they disappear, never to return—well, I think you have just saved yourself a lot of future heartaches. Be very glad they are no longer in your life.

Meant to Be

*W*e never really know

*I*f things are meant to be

*T*ill these precious things

*H*ave fled to where things flee.

*A*nd when they finally go

*L*ike petals in mid flight

*L*ife will show you—if these things were wrong or right.

*M*oving you to tears—or the brightest smile,

*Y*our world has yet to see in quite a while.

*H*enceforth, just know that things

*E*ach thing that breeds concern

*A*t times may spread its wings

*R*etreat and then sojourn

*T*o dwell off in the distance …

*… So by all means set them free,
and if a thing returns. Then it was meant to be.*

—***Tony Haynes***

Dating after Divorce

Chapter 6

Preparing for Your Date

What to Wear

While preparing for any date, one crucial task is deciding what to wear. Of course, you should dress appropriately for the activity in a dignified manner. Something many people don't consider is keeping track of what they wore and when. You may think I'm silly right now, but how would you feel if this happened to you: During the fifth date, you realize the shirt you are wearing was worn on the first and third date with the same person. They might wonder if you own any other clothes.

To make dressing for dates a little easier, I have picked out a few specific outfits based on activity types. One example is my first-date dress. On any first date where it is appropriate to wear a dress, I wear this one. The black dress is sleeveless but easily works with a jacket. I can wear it just about any time of day and in any season or weather condition.

Keeping a clothing log will also assist you in dressing for success. These logs are simple to make but keep a different log for each person you are trying to impress. On the top of the page, put the person's name. Make three columns under their name: the left is the calendar date, the middle column the activity, and in the far right, list what you wore.

This is a little trick that has served me well not only in dating but in my professional life as well. The field I worked in was mostly male, and people never noticed what suit the male district managers wore, but they did notice if the women wore the same outfit on consecutive visits. For more on looking and feeling your best after divorce, please see the second book in this series: *Divorced and Scared No More: Practical Advice for the Newly Divorced.*

To Ring or Not to Ring?

I wore a wedding ring on my left hand for twenty-six years. After my divorce, I thought I was smart by wearing a black onyx ring on that same finger. My hand just felt naked if I didn't have a ring on it.

I have a good male friend named Doug. We go out sometimes, and he is my "wingman," and I am his "wing woman." It's nice to go out with a friend of the opposite sex with no expectations. If you don't meet anyone new while you are out together, you have each other to dance with and have a fun evening. On occasion, there may be someone else around you who you might want to get rid of, and that wing-person may just come in handy and take care of them quickly.

You know ladies when it comes to our boy "friends," we don't notice their actions as we would those of the guy we consider as a "boyfriend." One evening, I decided to start watching Doug more carefully than usual. Every so often, an attractive woman would walk through the door, and I noticed Doug turning his head. The first few times, I thought he was checking out the lovely ladies. I also saw some very nice-looking women who had noticed Doug, but when they walked by our table, he didn't even look up at them. I started thinking, "What is up with this otherwise intelligent man?"

I had to ask Doug if there was something women needed to know about men. I said, "When we first came in this place, you were like a hawk checking out the room. Within five minutes, you could tell me every woman who had your attention. Then, whenever a new woman came in, you looked, but when they walked by, you didn't even look up. Why?" His answer was something I had never thought about until he said, "If a woman has a ring of any type on her ring finger, I'm not interested."

Men can see from across the room if there is a ring, and they don't care what type it is. Doug's view is that if there is a ring, the woman is engaged, separated, newly divorced, widowed, or married. The ring is like a beacon saying she is attached in some way to someone else. He doesn't want to waste his time with a woman who is not completely available.

Then I pulled out my left hand from under the table and showed him my little black onyx ring. He very sternly looked at me and said, "Take that thing off!" I guess guy friends don't notice girl "friends" the same way they notice potential "girlfriends."

Advice to Keep in Mind for Your Meet and Greet or the First Date

You have planned a meet and greet or the first date. If you're like many of us, the question is, "Now what do I do on a date? I haven't been on a date in years!" But this is going to be your year, and you are ready. We all get a little intimidated on a first date. Especially if you have been out of the dating world for a while. It is even harder to get back in the swing of things. Here are some tips I used for my first dates.

- **Keep your expectations realistic:** We all have flaws, and you and your date are no exceptions. Ask yourself these three questions after your first date: Do I like them? Are they easy to talk to, and do I feel comfortable? Is there any attraction? If you answer yes to these questions, get a second date.
- **Follow your gut because it is usually right:** Pay close attention to anything that makes you uncomfortable.
- **Dress appropriately and with dignity:** Be presentable, neat, well-groomed, and choose business casual clothes. Strive to look like the guy or girl next door and someone whom they would feel comfortable bringing home to their parents.
- **Remind yourself how great you are:** Leave all your negative thoughts at home and think about all you have to offer. For more on creating a positive self-image, please check out the first book in this series (*Divorced and Scared No More: Emotional Support for the Newly Divorced*).
- **Etiquette is not just a word; use your manners!** It is truly the golden rule of dating, even if you are not interested in the date. Please display good manners. Etiquette is not just a word—it is a lifestyle that needs to be followed. Always treat people the way you wish to be treated. Manners are important; unless you were raised in the wild, you should understand basic table manners. Do not shovel your food in

your mouth, eat off your date's plate, try to feed them, pick at your teeth, and so on.

- o Manners are not just about how you behave at the table. Showing good manners includes not talking about your previous relationships or anyone else you may be dating. Don't comment on the attractiveness of others in the restaurant or have a wandering eye. We all have cell phones, but it is rude to talk or text on your phone while on a date. Unless you need the phone on for a babysitter to contact you, turn it off, or at least set it to silent. Your date should be the center of your attention.

- **Be on time for your date:** There is nothing worse than waiting for a first date to show up. Your date will be sitting wondering if you have stood them up or if you're just stuck in traffic. First dates are stressful enough; don't add to the stress by being late.
- **Only talk about yourself for 50 percent of the time:** The conversation should not be about how wonderful you are and everything you have accomplished. Accept compliments and talk about the things in your life you are proud of—briefly. Point out your good qualities and accomplishments, but do not brag. You don't need to give your date a résumé of your entire life. Make sure to ask your date about their accomplishments and compliment them as well.

- **Show them encouraging body language:** Lean toward them when they talk, make eye contact, and smile. If you like them, you will probably already be doing these things naturally.
- **Be considerate when you order:** Look for something at a mid-range price point, or ask them what they are ordering, and then choose something at the same price or less. If your date orders an appetizer or starter salad, order something as well, so you will be eating at the same time (It's always awkward to wonder, "Do I start eating or wait for their food to get here?"). This same rule of thumb goes for cocktails. If you decide to order a drink, limit yourself to one or two; it can get expensive quickly, and under no circumstances should you get tipsy. Don't order messy items, like spaghetti, or things you have to eat with your hands. Be sure not to order stuff with lots of herbs; you don't want anything to get stuck in your teeth and not know it is there. If your date is not ordering something with garlic and onions, skip those items on the first date.

Additional advice specifically for a blind date:
- **Come prepared with friendly conversation:** Don't write up a script, but consider what you might talk about. If possible, find out from your mutual friend what kind of things your date does in their free time. Make connections by talking about some of those activities. Of course, be ready

to talk about yourself a little bit as well, but keep it light and positive.

- **Leave expectations out of it:** If you go into a blind date looking for your future partner, it's unlikely to go well. You will be looking for Mr. or Ms. Perfect and will be on the lookout for flaws. Your date is likely to have some flaws, as do you. Instead, look at the date as meeting a friend for a fun time out. This takes the pressure off, making you open to discovering who they are and the qualities they have as a person, not as a potential mate.

These little tips can help you with that first date or meet and greet. After a while, you won't be intimidated at all, and you will view your first date as a chance to learn about a new friend. Keep the topics light, pleasant, and positive. Ask about hobbies and things they are passionate about in their life. Make sure you listen to what they have to say and ask questions. Avoid taboo topics like religion, politics, or money. Be yourself and have a sense of humor; remember it's their first date with you, too.

Let the Restaurant Help You

Gender has nothing to do with a person's intent or desire to cause harm to another. Let the restaurant help you with your meet and greet or date.

When meeting someone for a meet and greet or the first date, I recommend you do a few things to protect yourself, especially if you have met the person online. If you can arrange for friends to be at the same meeting place, have them arrive ahead of you so that they can watch over you until you feel it's safe for them to leave. For many of us, though, this is not an available option. When I am on my own, I try to stop in or call the restaurant ahead of time. I let them know that I'll be at the restaurant on a date with someone I don't know; if it is an Internet date, I tell them that, too.

I request they seat us as close to the middle of the restaurant as possible and at a table or booth that is only for two. It will create a comfortable distance between you and your date. If you are seated in the middle of the room, they are less likely to do anything inappropriate.

When I arrive, I make sure the hostess knows who I am, and I verify that everyone is aware of the situation. If they are not aware, I make sure to explain everything to them. Then I ask if they would please let the waitress or waiter know that if I need any help, I will ask the server a question like, "Wasn't that game on Saturday great?" At that point, they know I will excuse myself from the table, and they will delay my date with the payment of the bill or something else while I leave.

Last but not least, since the staff is aware of my situation, if they notice anything, they feel I should be mindful of, they can tell me there is a call for me at the office or bar. When I go up to get the "call," they can say to me their concerns. If the staff thinks they need to tell you something, you need to listen. On three occasions, I have been delighted I had these precautions in place because they helped me to make a safe and polite exit.

Many of you may say you would be embarrassed to do such a thing. Just think for one moment how you would feel if what happened to a friend of mine happened to you. She did not take my advice, and even though she felt uncomfortable with her date, she was still polite to the man and let him walk her to her car. He followed her home, and she did not notice that she was being followed. The next morning, as she came out to get in her car to go to work, she saw the man waiting behind her car. Luckily for her, the neighbors noticed, came over, and the man quickly left.

Just think of all the other things that could have happened. So, don't be embarrassed to be in cahoots with the restaurant. The people I have approached have all been more than willing and pleased to help me. In fact, I get many comments like, "You go, girl." Some have also told me that they have had Internet dates and think this is a good idea and started using it themselves.

Within a few days after your date, go to the restaurant and thank them, and if you can afford it, give them a tip. If you can't afford a tip, take something like candy, homemade cookies, or cupcakes to let them know you appreciate their help.

A Few Don'ts While Dating

Here are a few little things you should not do while dating after a divorce. Following these don'ts will help you have a much more enjoyable dating experience.

- Don't spend the whole day getting ready for the date. Too much of a buildup will set you up for a letdown.
- Don't spend more than four hours on your first date. You need to leave your date and yourself wanting to spend more time with one another and wanting to learn more about each other.
- Don't call, text, or email your date repeatedly, either before or after the date.
- Don't stop dating other people after just one date with someone. This is not the freeway to your next relationship. Have fun and learn about yourself and what you want in a partner.
- Don't overanalyze everything. It is just a date and nothing more.
- Don't introduce your kids to your dates. Children must not be involved until you are in a serious relationship.
- Don't let your date know where your home is for a few dates. Drive yourself to dates until you both have gotten to know one another better. If after a few dates you decide this is not the right person for you, it is easier to end things if they do not know your home address.
- Don't take rejection after a few dates to heart; just accept that the person wasn't right for you and move on.

Talk and Get to Know Who You're Dating

After you have decided to make your relationship exclusive, take time, and talk to get to know who you're dating. Make sure you're getting to know important details of each other's lives, and date intentionally. Here are a few of the types of things to ask or discuss with your new partner. Finding out someone is not a good match for you is always better earlier rather than later.

- Discuss your beliefs, both those from childhood and your current views.
- Talking about upbringing can reveal a lot about how your partner sees the world and what he or she believes a healthy relationship should include.
- Discuss the physical aspect of your relationship. If you're ready to have sex and your partner is waiting for marriage, the situation can be awkward if you're not on the same page.
- Discuss your thoughts on relationships, commitment, and how you'd define where you are currently at and where you would like to be in the future.
- It can be hard to see how someone will handle a disagreement until you've had your first fight. Discussing previous conflicts can help both of you understand how each of you will deal with conflict.
- What does your partner love to do the most? Can you share this activity, and can they share your favorite activity?
- Make sure that you get to know your partner's friends. People

are a reflection of the company they keep.

- What does your partner do on the nights you're not together? Their social life when you are not around is a clue to who they are as a person.
- Is your partner a spender or a saver? As many of you know, arguments over money and sex are two driving forces behind divorce. Be transparent about your spending habits and talk about how you each handle your finances.
- Are you heading in the same direction as far as your dreams and goals? Where do you each view yourselves in five, ten, or more years? Sharing dreams and goals can better help you assess whether you and your partner can thrive in a relationship.

The Greatness of Just Being

*B*irds don't want to be flowers;

*E*lephants don't want to be rain;

*I*slands just want to be islands;

*N*ot a Jim, a

*G*eorge or a Jane.

*S*tars don't want to be oceans;

*P*aradise will never complain;

*I*t's the greatness of just being

*R*emaining the you, you remain.

*I*t's not always about becoming,

*T*hough to become is the

*U*ltimate fate.

*A*ccepting the greatness of being

Lets you be who you are and be great.
— *Tony Haynes*

Chapter 7

Dating Challenges

Dump the Checklist, but Don't Settle

What on Earth would be the point in settling for someone you are not totally in love with or could enjoy as a lifelong partner? That is like asking if you would still eat chocolate even if you couldn't taste anything. Why even bother having a relationship in the first place? It is a sure sign that you are settling for someone when you shouldn't be. When you say things like, "This is my chance," "I just don't want to be alone," "I'm tired of dating," or "there are billions of people in this world, and I could learn to love anyone," more likely than not, it is not about the person you are with at all. It's about you, and how you see yourself, your own issues, or your own fears. I'm not saying specifically you—this is true of most people.

Here is a better system than the failed checklist option you used the last go-around when looking for a mate. You know, the one that didn't work out so well for you? You are here now, and welcome aboard. As I wrote earlier in this book, dump the checklist and just set your deal breakers. Try not to assume there will be problems with a person based on first impressions. Instead, allow problems to manifest themselves before you decide whether or not to continue to date.

Don't sit across the table from dates, trying to figure out what's wrong with them. Take the time to get to know them, and don't be too critical on the first date. Everyone is nervous here, so allow enough time to observe them in their natural, comfortable state. Learn their virtues and vices. Let them be themselves and make sure you are who you are, your true self. With time, you both will learn each other's quirks. Sometimes they are deal-breakers, and other times they become things you love the most about your partner. It isn't flashy or glitzy, but it's a pretty good system, and it gives both of you the time to make a fair assessment.

Remember everything does not have to be 100 percent perfect. You can love your partner 100 percent for the person they are, the real, flawed human being that we all are. Thinning hair, a bit older, a crazy ex—we all have baggage and shortcomings, but don't let them distract you from a potential relationship.

One last note: Do not make a mental list of all the things you could change in this person because it never works. I have found the true virtue of finding your mate is learning to accept everything about them as-is. If there are quirks about them that you cannot take, then you need to move on. The problem doesn't lie in their faults; the problem lies in your inability to accept them for who they are. The only change that you should focus on is within yourself. That is the only way you will find true love and happiness.

Run from the Always-Right Person

Get the facts first. You can distort them later.
—Mark Twain

One man, I dated told me the first night I met him that he was always right, no ifs, buts, or maybes. I thought he was joking since he even laughed when he said it. Well, oh my, he was serious. Come to think of it; my ex-husband used to say he was always right. Maybe there is a trend there: I need to learn from so I can avoid making the same mistake again.

Both men, if we ever disagreed, would push their points even if they knew they were wrong. They did not apologize without blaming me. The closest they came to an admission that they may have been wrong was something like, "I did not explain it well enough" or "I didn't have all the information." Being able to admit that you are wrong and take responsibility for your actions is a sign of maturity. This type of arrogant person is not willing to negotiate at any time for any reason. A person who does not compromise can be hard to deal with most of the time.

Being in a relationship is an excellent way for people to discover new things about themselves. Since everyone is different, you continuously have to adjust yourself to the other person. But if your partner is unwilling to adapt himself or herself to you, you will find yourself changing more and more about you for them. Relationships require compromise, not conformity. This type of person is very good at manipulating you. They make you feel like every problem the two of you have is your fault. They cannot do the littlest of things to show they want to be with you.

One example of a person failing to be considerate toward you is if they are repeatedly late for dates with you. It starts as an occasional issue but soon turns into the regular pattern. They say they are running late because of their job, or kids, but just about everything is more important than being on time for you. Then the calls to tell you they will be late stop, and you are expected to be ready whenever they do show up. Everything they want to do is more important than you, but you are expected to be available when it is convenient for them. If you are not there when it is suitable for them, they blame you, saying you are not making them a priority.

This constant blame game isn't healthy, and you shouldn't have to deal with it. Who wants to be with a person who you must often wait for, who places all the blame on you and makes it seem like everything's your fault anyway?

I know this may come as a real shock to you, but some people genuinely do think they are always right or cannot admit that they made a mistake. I don't know what it is, but there is something deep in the heart of this kind of person that will not let them admit that they do not know everything.

> *When I eventually met Mr. Right, I had no idea that his first name was Always.*
> —Rita Rudner

Learn the Art of Walking Away and Saying No

Now that you are confident and happy with your life. Along with who you have become after your journey of processing your divorce Stop and think for a moment: Other than the way we meet people, has dating changed as much as everyone says?

I think I stumbled upon this question because I was afraid to date again and to even possibly open my heart to love. I had not dated in over twenty years, and the idea of dating felt bizarre, so I did what any good business person would do: I treated my dates as a business dinner. At the end of my dates, I would shake a man's hand, and for some reason, they became more interested in me. Then I noticed something else. When I went out with friends and met a new man, I would talk to the man for a bit, having a nice, yet short, conversation, and then excuse myself to go back to my group. As the night went by, I would stop and chat again for just a bit. I noticed the men seemed to be much more interested every time I went by to see if I would stop again and have another conversation. If I did not come back near them after a while, they would come and find me to start another short chat. I realized they did not look at me as a prude, but as a challenge.

Because I had become a challenge, men seemed to agree with everything I wanted to do. Then one evening, I had a date with a man I had become very interested in recently. Davis wasn't my type when I met him; I thought he was a nice guy, but no big deal. The more I got to know him, the more attractive he became to me. I don't know about you, but if I become emotionally attracted to a man, they become more and more physically attractive to me, as well. Then one evening we had a date, and we were deciding some of the details of what we were going to do. I preferred to go to the clubhouse at the golf course, but Davis looked at me and told me "no" with a half-smile on his face. Without realizing it, I had grown a little spoiled and quite accustomed to the treatment of the other men saying "yes."

When he said, "no," I thought, "How dare you? Men don't tell me that." Then the bells went off in my head: The reason this man had become so attractive to me was that he didn't do everything I wanted, and he told me "no."

When I was in high school, a boy at the local car wash kept asking me out, and I kept saying "no." He was a very popular boy from the school district next to mine. Girls pursued him regularly, and he was not accustomed to someone not wanting to date him. The more I refused to go on a date with him, the more determined he became to find out more about me from people at my school and by going to eat at the restaurant where I worked. One day on my way to work, I went to get the car washed, and he turned off the whole thing when the brushes were next to my doors. Scott then said, "I won't turn the carwash on until you agree to go out with me." After a few choice words, and finally realizing I would be late for work, I agreed to meet him at a neighboring restaurant after work with my friends. That date was the beginning of a very long courtship and my first love; I almost married that man.

Dating now is the same as when we were young. We want what we have to work to get. We all enjoy the challenge. Make sure you are a challenge but not an unreachable one.

Single Again and Again and ...

Do you have the short-term curse since your divorce—your relationships inexplicably go away after a few months, and all of a sudden, you're single again? Regardless of exactly how hard you try; do you find you cannot get past just a short-term relationship? Does this leave you feeling like you have an expiration date? Dating failure can be very distressing. If dating isn't working out for you, reevaluate your dating habits. Have you ever considered that maybe you are the problem, not the relationship? You don't intend to make the very same choices again and again, but do you? If you are single again, attempt to evaluate your choices, decisions, and actions and learn from them to avoid future relationships ending as the last one did.

Review your last few relationships and see if there are any similarities. Were your partners the same type of person? Did you rush into the relationships too quickly? Discuss your past relationships with your friends and see if collectively, you can come up with areas to make changes in your life. Learn how to choose potential partners differently.

When you were young, invincible, vibrant, and you knew you could get a date, you could get around the dating world with ease. When you are more mature (this is my viewpoint), your physique is very rarely the same after a few little ones, and your looks aren't quite the same, either, yet being more mature and single again is far more beneficial than the advantages of youth.

I have confidence knowing I will be fine on my very own, knowing that I don't need to depend on another person to survive, and knowing that if I choose to go out, I can buy my very own darn drinks, dinner, and perhaps my date's as well. I also know that I don't need to be so consumed about my looks, either, because I know I am a vibrantly beautiful, mature lady with self-worth that I have earned throughout my life. Regardless of outside packaging, beauty does come from within, and when you believe in yourself, you become a real beauty! That assurance cannot be found in any potion out there on any shelf, and it is wisdom that comes with age. Selecting a partner should not mean randomly choosing the first potential partner who walks past. It should mean picking a person who complements us and makes us happy. Many feel they are not able to be single in life or believe they don't have time for the meeting process that is necessary to find the ideal spouse. You must participate in this process to ensure you don't end up single again in a few weeks or months.

Enjoy being single. Take time to do what you desire when you desire it, and with whom you want to be around. Be grateful that you're not stuck in a relationship that was not for you. Do not stop trying to find your dream relationship, but stop making the same choices that are not right for you. Change your view of dating to see it as merely a brand-new method to meet new friends. Enjoy your own company and learn the difference between being alone and being lonely.

Dealing with Dating Burn-Out

Have you ever thought to yourself, "Are there any normal people out there to date?" That is the way I feel right now. At times, I think, "All of these people are single for a reason." Then I remember, "I am one of those people, and I am normal." I am not sure what the reason is, but I seem to attract some of the more "colorful" people as dates. Most of the time I laugh it off, but after a while I get the dreaded dating burn out. We all know the symptoms, like dreading even going on a date or all the effort it seems to take emailing, texting and chatting, only to find out that all that time wasted on yet another person with zero partner potential.

It is no surprise when dating burnout happens. I understand one of the prevailing views is to keep dating when burnout hits. I think if we keep pushing ourselves to date, it will make the dating burnout worse. Here are some strategies that I use to get over the burnout.

- **Recharge:** It's okay to stay home for a short time to recharge. The first step is to get back out there and have fun when you are ready. That doesn't mean you have to date, but at least get out of the house, be with people, do things, hang out with friends, and have a good time.

- **Stop looking:** Now is the time to stop dating or looking for a partner. Dating should be fun; it should not feel like a job. Take the time to recharge your batteries. Once the pressure is off and you start living your life again, you will attract more people to be around you.

- **Choose new activities:** Find something that you have always wanted to do but did not have the time for and do it. Try to list at least three things you enjoy doing, and then throw yourself into those activities. Make sure at least two of these activities are not solo activities. Maybe join a poker club like Texas Hold 'Em; or if you love reading, join a book club; or if shooting a gun is something you enjoy, join a shooting range, and so on. Some of the bonuses can be meeting new people, keeping busy, losing yourself in the project, and building your confidence.

- **Reflect:** Reevaluate your feelings to make sure you are not the problem. Reflect to see if all the baggage in your past has been fully processed. Past wounds must be completely healed, or without knowing it, you may be making the same mistakes over and over. Are your dates just carbon copies of your ex with different names? Unless you take some time to figure out what you are feeling, your love life will seem to be stuck on repeat. Help is out there; do not be too proud to receive it. I am pleased and proud to say I got help when I needed it, and I do know I am a more confident person because of the therapy I received.

- **Connect with opposite-sex friends:** Take one of your friends of the opposite sex out to dinner, a movie, or dancing, making sure to laugh and have fun. It is helpful to share your feelings and get a hug from someone of the opposite sex. Your friends can fill the void, and there are no unrealistic expectations.

- **Regain your self-confidence:** Take time for yourself and banish the negativity and start boosting your confidence.

When the time is right, and your batteries have recharged, someone will ask you out, and you will want to go, or you will walk up to the computer and decide to look online again.

Getting Out of Dating Burnout

If you are ready to re-join the dating world, here are a few steps that can assist you in getting out of dating burnout.

A date is just a date, so go out and have fun. View it as an opportunity to meet a new friend, have a nice meal, or have a bowl of ice cream or a cup of coffee. Often people have all kinds of hopes, dreams, and expectations before they even go on a date. So often I hear people saying, "On the way to the date, I thought they were the one I was going to have a relationship with." Face it: That probably isn't the case. Remember that the only person in control of what you do and how you feel is you. Don't put your happiness in someone else's hands. It's best to relax and enjoy the other person's company. Relax. If you feel a little nervous, smile, realizing they are probably also a little nervous. Did you know a smile can be a little sexy and contagious? This person might end up being someone you enjoy spending time more with in the future, even if it is just as a friend.

Learn not to take rejection personally. Not everyone you go out on a date with is right for you. Understand you are also not right for everyone you meet. The date is no big deal. It's a process. You like to drink your tea, and I'll enjoy my coffee. Sometimes you will find yourself coming home from a date laughing because you were total opposites. Once a man and I started laughing about how opposite we were on the date, and because of that odd date, we became terrific friends who enjoy debating about everything.

Usually, you should limit your deal-breakers to three or four, but since you have gone through dating burnout (or had your emotions toyed with), seven to ten would be okay for a short time. Remember this is only for a temporary period because you need to get yourself back out there. View this phase, like walking before you run. Learn to walk a little bit more carefully, be a little bit more selective, and choose people who you can feel relaxed around. As you become more confident, reduce the list back to your regular three or four deal breakers. This increase is only to help you while you transition back to your usual fun dating self.

I hate to break it to you, but you may need to change the type of people you are dating. Look long and hard, and see if the type you were choosing were the right type for you. Dating the wrong kind of person might be why you feel burned out or why you were getting your heart played with like a dog's chew toy. People who are successful at dating and getting out of dating burnout are the ones who understand dating needed a change. It is another step, so again, don't take it so seriously and don't compare dates to someone you dated in the past. With the right type of attitude and expectations, you will appreciate this new phase and once again reflect on the things you have learned about yourself.

Even if you put these tips into action, the dating world is going to throw you left turns, loops, and curves, then send you up hills and down hills, so learn to go with the flow. Think of it as a little roller coaster; jump on and enjoy the ride. It's a crazy world out there, so take deep breaths, go to yoga class, call a friend, take a nap, go for a walk, go on a few dates, and then one day you'll find that last first date—but remember to enjoy the rollercoaster!

May Freedom Fall in Love with You

*M*ay freedom fall in love with you,

*A*nd may you always be free,

*N*ever bound by anything—except what you're bound to be.

*D*ance in light of discovery;

*E*xpedite enlightenment leading to

*L*iving a life in love with freedom,

*A*nd may freedom fall in love with you.

—Tony Haynes

Chapter 8

Important Points to Remember When Dating

Don't Bring Your Ex on Your Date

Our past haunts us all, no matter how much effort we make toward leaving our history in our past. Trust me, the Ghost of Your Ex Past is no *Christmas Carol.* Without realizing it, many individuals develop an inclination to hightail it away from people who in the slightest way, remind them of their ex-spouse. It's not the best way to react when you go out trying to find a new healthy relationship. If you end a relationship, take the time to see if this could have been one of the factors. If so, you may have a little more healing to do. Just because a person is a vegetarian does not mean they are just like your ex, though it does mean they probably will not enjoy a date at a steakhouse — just a little tip.

Marni Battista, relationship coach and founder of Dating with Dignity, offers an incredibly good signal that you are ready to consider another romantic relationship: It is whenever you realize you can talk about your ex, and it doesn't involve referring to him or her in a negative way.

If you are on a date with a divorced person, be observant and sensitive because as you know, many divorced people are more fragile than they look. Their relationship ended for a reason, and it is quite possible it ended very badly. Watch closely for your date's reactions to the topics you bring up, simply because you might mention an issue that is funny to you personally but might remind your date of some horrible memories. Always respond to signals to stop. You may not know this individual well, and despite what everyone says, all of us have bruises and baggage if we are alive and divorced. It is merely a fact of being divorced—or living life for that matter.

Do not talk about your ex on dates unless your date inquires or it is absolutely necessary. If you must discuss them, avoid negative comments. It is advisable to eliminate negativity from your life entirely and concentrate on getting it right the next time around (for more help with this, see the first book in this series: *Divorced and*

Scared No More: Emotional Support for the Newly Divorced). Under no circumstances, refer to your ex as the "love of your life." If you do, I am sure the date will end in a short time.

If you were married for an extended period, while talking about your life, you might find yourself accidentally talking about your ex. A little tip I use when referring to your past. Instead of saying, "when we went to the Grand Canyon," I say, "when I went to the Grand Canyon." It is difficult to eradicate your ex out of your life. Nevertheless, you do not want your date thinking the remainder of their time together with you is going to be spent discovering everything you did with your ex. Another reason never to mention your ex is that sometimes you may well be saying points you didn't like about your ex and your date could be thinking, "but I enjoy doing that, so I guess we can't be a couple." People often tell me they always hated doing a specific activity with their ex like hiking, but these days it is among the favorite activities they enjoy sharing with their new partner. Possibly it was the ex-factor mixed into the activity that prevented them from enjoying the experience.

Missing Physical Aspects of a Relationship

With the loss of any long-term relationship, you will encounter things you start to miss, such as a loving hug from a member of the opposite sex or a smile when a person watches you walk up. Many of us are lonely and miss having someone to wake up next to in the morning, a person who will hold us when we wake from a bad dream, and someone to share our fears and joy. We miss having a partner. The doubt and thoughts of "Will I be alone forever?" creep in.

You must put your past in the past and learn from the mistakes of your last relationship. Realize what a unique gem you are and believe it. Just because you do not have a partner does not make you lonely. Missing the physical aspects of a relationship is normal, but stay true to your values.

How you handle these feelings could send you down a wrong path if you are not careful. Fortunately, soon after my divorce, an excellent friend sat me down and said, "Guard against becoming ripe for the picking." I did not know what he meant (picking overripe fruit?), so he explained that I would meet individuals who would identify me as vulnerable and attempt to benefit from the situation. He warned me that everybody experiences it, and I must be able to self-identify whenever I begin to feel vulnerable. Now if I start feeling lonely or miss those small things I enjoyed in a relationship, I involve myself more at my religious, social group. It is nice to enjoy visiting with a group of friends who don't have any relationship expectations. The men within my group meet me with a big smile when I walk up to them, followed by a friendly hug. I do believe they miss those little things, too.

Numerous divorced people decide to "just go for it," and as a consequence, start to feel uncomfortable or perhaps slightly violated due to their rushed attempt at physical closeness. Others, who have not been touched in some time, are afraid of what their reactions might be if they do get touched and suppress virtually any touching or bodily contact. Either of these examples probably sends out the wrong message regarding who you are. Your date may think you are easy and you are just there for sex, but if you have no contact, they may think you are not considering any physical element in a romantic relationship; neither is an attractive scenario.

Okay, so what is the answer to this awkward problem? Some individuals believe touching a date in the slightest way when they first meet them is undoubtedly an absolute no-no. That is not true. To create a positive, strong first impression that will create an instantaneous bond with a date, casually and gently touch the outer side of their arm, while verbally expressing something appropriate. A touch on the outer side of the arm is not intimate enough to feel strange or out-of-place, but it's a clear-cut sign you are a personable, socially adept person. Be willing to give it a chance.

Unfortunately, many individuals might have sex early in a relationship simply because they miss sharing a physical experience with someone. As soon as the sex is over, they realize they rushed into it, and it was with the wrong person. Instead of gaining knowledge from their mistake, they decide it is vital to undertake a relationship with the person simply because they had sex because they are not the type of person who has sex with just anyone. So you made a mistake; every divorced person has made a minimum of one mistake (your ex is certainly one that comes to mind). Now pick up and move forward with your life and do not compound the problem with another mistake by starting a romantic relationship based on the fact that you had sex.

There are several issues you will need to examine before you decide to have sex for the first time with a new partner. Be sure you are emotionally, physically, mentally, and spiritually ready for any physical experience. You must also be practical and secure in the knowledge of what your view regarding sex is. Stick to your values and beliefs. Not what anyone tells you that you are supposed to do or think. Furthermore, I am sure you are aware of the possible dangers that can be linked to sexual activity, including unwanted pregnancy or sexually transmitted diseases or infections.

Amy Laurent, author, skilled matchmaker, and relationship expert, suggests an individual should typically wait eight weeks before having sexual intimacy. She also adds, "It is imperative to go slow and build a foundation before having sex. It does change things and will add in a more complicated dynamic if you have sex too early."

Here's an idea: Do not kiss on the first date! That's right, I said, do not kiss them. Yeah, you heard me. I will repeat it: Do not kiss on the first date. Ooh! I already said it a second time! When he or she zooms in, looking for that end-of-the-date kiss, turn and allow one on your cheek, or you could give a date one on his or her cheek. Pat them on the arm and tell them they need to work just a little harder for your kiss as you smile and give them a wink. Do not forget while leaving to request that they contact you to get together again sometime soon.

If a Friend Says, "Don't Date Them," Listen

In the dating world, there are many methods for meeting potential dates. Only about 5 percent of people meet in clubs. Many people are now using speed dating or online dating sites, but there are also the tried and tested ways we depended on before the Internet: for example, meeting people at church, through mutual friends, or some other activities.

For me, one meeting that comes to mind was at a dinner party at a friend's home. If you find yourself, as I did, meeting someone and sparks appear to fly, slow down and make time to do what I wish I had done. My friend came straight out and said, "Do not date him." She even went so far as texting him during the party to tell him to go away and leave me alone. She had known the person since college, and her husband had known him since grade school; they were, therefore, excellent judges of his character. At the time, I believed she was overprotective, so I did not invest time and ask her why she said those things. Yep. That would have been the smart thing to do.

If you meet someone via a friend, particularly when the friend has already known them for a long time, listen carefully if your friend informs you, they have concerns about you dating the individual. Realize they know them much better than you do, and in all probability, know each of your personalities and deal breakers very well. They probably have some information they're struggling to share that may help save you from heartache in the foreseeable future.

If you do choose to pursue the relationship, you will be entering into it with all the information, not what your potential date decides is pertinent. With all the necessary information, you most likely will not believe all of the spin the individual you happen to be dating might place on his or her past.

Judging an individual by the company they keep is merely part of the equation. All of us have friends who we were close to when we were younger, but as time passed and values changed, we became less involved in each other's lives. My friends and the person I was interested in were still friends, even though their lives have gone in different directions. My friend and her husband are very involved with their children and church. Their faith is the center of their home, but the gentleman I dated is what people call a C and E—you know, the kind of person who only practices their faith on Christmas and Easter. On all the other days of the year, fishing, football, and drinking all day are his priorities. The core of the friendship is still there for my friends and this gentleman, but it is now a result of shared history, not shared interests.

Simply because you respect and value the individual who introduced you does not necessarily mean their "old" friend has similar values. Take time to listen carefully to what your friend has to say or in some cases, avoid answering your questions.

Make Dating Fun

Here are a few additional thoughts to keep in mind while dating that can make your experience more enjoyable.

- Each date is another opportunity to find out more about what you do and do not want in your new life. Treat every date like a prospective new friend. If everything does not go very well on the dating front, you might find that you have a new partner in crime or a partner for salsa lessons (But not real crime, hopefully. Real salsa lessons are okay.). This date might not be a good match for you but could be perfect for a friend. My friend Julian is my partner for salsa dancing, meeting to see a movie, or going to the beach for a picnic. We didn't click when we tried dating each other, but we are great friends. God could have had us go on that date so that eventually, because we are friends, one of us might find our Mr. or Ms. Right.
- Ask your date questions! It shows that you are genuinely interested, and their opinion matters. It is always a good icebreaker, especially if a friend has introduced you and given you a few topics that would be good to discuss.
- Keep dating other people after only a few dates with someone. Have fun and learn about yourself and what you want in a partner. I wish there were another word for this phase that is about getting to know yourself and meeting new

people, but alas, society has dumped it all into this one big pot called dating.

- Stop over-analyzing everything. It is just a date, and nothing more.
- Look at your date, not at everyone else in the restaurant or the door. If you are worried about who might see you on your date, then that is a good clue that you probably are not ready to be dating. Your attention should be on your date and no one else.
- Don't date your cell phone. It sounds ridiculous, but US English Siri can be a true temptress, and UK English Siri (the one I have) can be a Casanova. Do not go down that road. Put your phone away! Unless it is an emergency, everything else on your phone can wait. How about putting it on Do Not Disturb? You can use this setting so if it is a person on your favorites list or someone calls twice the call will come through.

Dating after divorce may feel strange, but go out to enjoy the date and have a good time. Your date may lead to romance, or you may not click, but you will not know until you go. You are single now, and your life is full of opportunities. Elton John puts it very well in his song "I'm Still Standing," and it can be better than it ever was because you are now a true survivor.

I Got My Feet Wet

I watched the waves roll in,

*S*tanding by the shore.

I counted them a while

*T*hen I lost count counting more.

*F*orgetting my whole purpose

*A*nd what my heart still craves.

*T*hat day I got caught up in the

*E*ndless stream of waves.

& the waves rolled in around me

*L*ike repayment of a sweet debt

*O*wing nothing I just danced—'cause at last I got my feet wet.

*V*owing then I have returned—many times back to the shore,

*E*ach time I get my feet wet ...

... *I count my blessings more & more.*

— ***Tony Haynes***

Chapter 9

The Dogs of Dating

[While I was working on the Divorced and Scared No More *series, William Kenly with me shared that the* Dogs of Life *are very much the same for men and women. Since I have shared a few of my dating stories, I have asked William to share some of his so you can see that we all have the same issues while dating after divorce, especially those of us who were out of the dating world for an extended period of time. Hopefully some of William's dating stories, along with mine,*

will help you to understand that you are not the first to go through dating adventures. Additionally, maybe some of these stories will give you the ability to take the curves in stride and learn to laugh and enjoy the lighter side of dating.
—Tasher]

This chapter has been excerpted from *The Dogs of Divorce* by William Kenly

When someone leaves, it's because someone else is about to arrive.
—Paulo Coelho

The realization was suddenly on me that dating was legal again, followed quickly by the realization that I had only the faintest idea how to do it. I was like a kid in a candy store. "If guys only knew," I said to myself, "how many women there are out there, just waiting for a decent guy to ask them out!" Where have all the guys gone? The ratio of available girls to available guys is easily 10:1. One woman told me that most of the guys out there are married or broken or gay.

Dating is for fun; relationships are work. And I didn't want a relationship. I needed to figure things out about myself first. Since my days in college, I had never *not* been in a relationship. I didn't need to marry, and I didn't want to marry. I wanted to enjoy life. I wanted to date many women. But first I needed to be comfortable again being with a woman. I not only didn't want to settle down again, I also wanted to *not* settle down again. About three dates into this scene, one of my friends explained that no woman wants to invest time in a guy who won't settle down. They may claim to just want friendship, but deep down, they all want more. Funny, I had not thought of it that way.

I started dating the way I took on most challenges: I made a list. I was a little disappointed that I only could think of five eligible women, but I also knew friends who had friends. And, of course, the new world of technology in 2001 was opening the doors to Internet dating. I resolved to become proficient at each approach.

Discussing women with a friend at work, the friend suggested that I try a little Grecian Formula to get some of the gray out. I looked at my forty-seven-year-old self in the mirror that night for what seemed like the first time. It was a bit of a shock. I saw the wrinkles where my now-bigger ears were pulling the skin on my cheeks down. And then there was the hair, always combed flat over to one side, always kept short. When it got longer, it would develop that bothersome wave in the front. My face was fatter, and when did I develop those jowls? I was a bit out of shape and weighed a bit more than I used to.

Well, we can work on some of that, I thought confidently.

One of the new things I acquired after the separation was a new barber. Lori, the new, wise barber, suggested that I let the curls on top do whatever they wanted to do. "You have gorgeous hair," she purred as she flipped the curls on top, trying to imagine a looser me. I liked her saying that, so on a lark, I did stop combing the top. And two surprising things happened. First, my hair liked to part on the right side instead of the left side where I had been parting it for forty-some years. Second, my hair liked to curl on top. I let it curl and stopped carrying a comb, and I felt freer.

At about the same time, I stopped carrying a watch. I noticed how LED clocks are on every appliance and electronic gadget. I was never without the time, and my wrist was free. The minimalist life is so attractive.

And I joined an online dating site called **MatchMaker.com**.

The First Date

I looked across the desk at the banker filling out my account forms. *Not bad,* I thought. There was some confusion in my mind about whether I should be dating before the divorce was final in a couple of months, but I sure was thinking about it. I wondered how to ask a woman out. I wondered what a date between two forty-somethings was like. The last time I dated a single woman was when I was a teenager, thirty years ago.

Her ring finger was bare.

"This job allows me to be home for my son and schedule my trips to the bank at my own convenience," she chatted. When I asked, she answered, openly enough, that she lived in Lynchville, a few towns over, so it was an easy drive. I didn't push it any further.

Three days later, when Linda called to tell me the loan had been approved, I pushed out the rehearsed sentence as though I were giving birth: "So maybe you would like to have lunch with me sometime?"

There! I said it! I wanted to add more, to sound casual, but I bit my tongue. And held my breath. And clenched my fists. And sank in my chair, almost into a fetal position. Waiting. Waiting. And waiting. How could she keep quiet so long? It was minutes! Hours! *She must hate me. I crossed the line. What an idiot I am!*

I prayed that no one came into my office while I was sitting with my eyes clenched, hunched over in my chair, holding my breath, listening to the silence on the other end of the phone. *Had she hung up? Why wasn't she answering?*

"I would enjoy that," her soft voice purred.

"What?" I silently screamed. "Yippee! Yahoo! I can't believe it!" screamed the banshee in my little-boy head.

"Good!" was all I could say out loud.

I don't remember anything else, except trying to control my exhalation so she wouldn't hear it. We agreed to talk more that night, and I hung up and floated across the office, afraid to leave my office until I could control my grin.

After long, protracted rejection and emotional abuse, it was easy to believe that I might be unworthy, or unattractive, or that I had some code word tattooed in special ink on my forehead that only women can read. Maybe it says, "Jerk!" or "Beware" or "Sick." To have a beautiful woman treat me as something desirable was an amazing feeling, a feeling I will never again forget.

The next day, I took a long lunch and drove to a quiet restaurant near the golf course. She was that day the most beautiful creature I had ever seen. What to say? The voices in my head vetoed every subject as quickly as I thought of them. Later, I could not remember talking at all. I remembered the winter sun coming in the window and making me uncomfortably hot. I was amazed that I was sitting there with a pretty woman. And she didn't think I was pond scum.

The next meeting was also a "safe" one: dinner with two of her friends, and then a hockey game at Yale.

We talked on the phone every night for the next week. We laughed about the lunch date, how I felt like a deer caught in the headlights, unable to move. She was funny and nice. She was more fun to be with every time we talked.

And talking was all we did. Neither of us wanted or knew how to handle more. We never even held hands.

She had a Master's degree in education, and I liked that, so I revised my online profile criteria to consider only those with a college education. It also struck me that I had spent most of my life simplifying and censoring my words so I would not step on a landmine of emotions. I realized that I was not used to having unguarded conversations. It was liberating.

One night on the phone, Linda asked me a question out of the blue. She apologized and asked if I smoked or had ever smoked. As I quickly put out my cigarette, my mind raced at warp speed, considering and rejecting alternative responses. She went on to explain that her husband had died of lung cancer three years before, and she could not deal with it again.

"Linda, the answer is 'yes,' although right now, I would give anything to give you a different answer. I quit several years ago and just started again with the divorce, and I can quit again for good."

"Oh no," she whispered. "I remember my husband going through the 'quitting routine,' and it is just so hard." After a pause she added with resolution, "I just cannot do that again." There was some other little talk. Some apologies. We wished each other well, and another door closed.

My mom always said, "One door never closes but another one opens."

It took about two days for the next door to open.

The Cable Lady

The cable company made an appointment to send a representative out to my condo that week to sign the papers for cable service, so I was not surprised when the security intercom rang and the voice announced itself as being from the cable company. What did surprise me was the very feminine sound of that voice.

We sat at my glass kitchen table. She was going through the cable channel options. I was thinking about what an interesting situation this was. She was good looking and well spoken, early thirties, tallish, with long blonde hair pulled into a bun. Couldn't see what kind of body she had past the heavy cable turtleneck sweater, but it seemed to be slender. And full. She had a long neck. I wondered what her story was that she would go into strange guys' apartments like this every night.

Without thinking about my motivations, or hers, and fresh from my successful contact with Linda, I asked, "Would you like to go see a show with me this weekend?" Sometimes I surprise myself—like just then. I wouldn't have blamed her if she just stood up and walked out of my condo. Or maybe stood up and slapped me and walked out of my condo. But inside I was feeling like a little kid with a new toy. Not that I would know what to do with this toy, but the answer would be "nothing" if I didn't try.

She stopped in the middle of the form she was filling out and looked at me with piercing blue eyes. I saw a faint smile at the corners of her mouth as she tried to figure out whether this was a good idea or not. I could only grin, a huge naive grin that I was sure she would interpret to mean that I was a sicko pervert. But I couldn't control it. "Okay. Call me tomorrow after noontime." She turned back to the forms, writing her home number on the top. "Now, do you want the Sports Channel?"

Why did I pick the Christmas sing-along? I thought as we walked into the Shubert Theater. Wrong. Wrong. Wrong. She was a good sport, but neither of us did much singing. At intermission, we went out and walked four or five New Haven blocks, smoking half a dozen cigarettes apiece. When her coat opened, I could see that she was not hiding her good form tonight. I was feeling confused. I was at a place that was not interesting to either of us with a person who surely, I was not allowed to be with (at least that's how it felt, after twenty-four years of marriage; I was sure someone would arrest me for infidelity). And I had no idea where I was driving this bus. And I was happy. We went back into the Christmas performance. Later I could not remember if we talked about anything at all. I did hold her arm as we walked. It felt good, but illegal. I glanced at the faces of passersby to see if anyone noticed that I was, or had recently been, a married man.

I drove her, in my minivan (not a "player's vehicle," she told me), back to her house in Belmont that she shared with a roommate named "Pink." Pink worked nights, but that's all the detail I was going to get. She had cats, and a house full of overstuffed furniture. As she gave me the tour of the house, and we wound up in the bedroom, I wondered why a beautiful woman would show a man she barely knew into her bedroom. The amusing part was, I really did not understand that she was signaling to me that she wanted to make love. I was too busy noticing that we both had the same model of GE alarm clock on our respective nightstands to consciously think about the possibilities right there at my fingertips. I still do not know to this day if I would have done anything differently.

We talked awhile in the living room. She had no siblings, and her folks were still in Sweden. She was thirty-three and had been here for five years. No college, but she spoke well. Unable to go forward that night, I knew I could only leave. As I got up, I felt a conscious, overwhelming sadness at not being physically close to anyone for a very long time. Without any shame, I hung my head and I pathetically asked her for a hug, which she freely gave in full measure, pressing her tall body—thighs, hips, full breasts—against all of me, and she rested her mouth on my neck, below my ear. She held me; maybe she felt sorry for me. Then, not knowing what to do, I turned and left. I think "pathetic" is one of the steps to happiness.

We saw each other once more. I tried to call her several times in the next few weeks. She answered sometimes, and we talked briefly. I knew it was probably a lost cause. I was beginning to feel the depths of my inability to function in a normal setting. I felt uninteresting and unable to carry on a conversation. The one good thing was that I did feel like I was moving on and trying to learn. There was forward motion.

That was about the time I started dedicating more time to online dating, and I was introduced to **Parents without Partners**. Each one was a portal to new experiences.

MatchMaker.com

The 9/11 Widow: One of the first profiles on the online dating website that caught my attention was a lady who wanted to talk instead of meeting just now. That was fine with me because she sounded intelligent, and I wanted to slow myself down a little. Online dating sites show the world many things about you, like when you are online. And she was always online, day in and day out, like she was listening for someone, even at 3 a.m.

On the third phone call, she said that she had recently lost her husband and everyone knew about the incident. She referred me to a website, and I suspected as I was going there that it was a 9/11 memorial site. Everyone has their own demons to wrestle with, and this was hers. She never wanted to meet, and we stopped messaging each other. But I never forgot that she was always online, day and night, ready to receive a message from someone who never called.

Years later, estranged from my kids, every time I opened my email or checked my cell for texts, I was hoping for some message from one of them, like the 9/11 lady, hoping that one day her husband, perhaps hurt and with amnesia but not dead, would contact her. And I hoped that one day, or in the middle of the night, one of my kids would finally contact me.

Parents without Partners

The wife of a friend from work called one day to say she had a bunch of girlfriends who had a loose organization called "**Parents without Partners.**" The group was mainly made up of women, but they tried to recruit men, too. Parents without Partners is for people who have no mate, usually due to divorce, but sometimes because of death. They get together every couple of weeks. She asked if I would like to come to the next meeting.

Two evenings later, a (male) friend from work and I walked into the Southport Brewery, an upscale, yuppie restaurant. The women were already there, all six of them filling up a booth. Introductions were made all around, and I sat in the middle on one side, my friend in the middle on the other. Five of the women were divorced, one never married. All but the never-married woman had school-age kids. A couple liked to ski; a couple had not been to one of these gatherings in a few months. I learned about "A" weekends and "B" weekends—if you have visitation with your kids every first and third weekend, then you do not want your girlfriend to have her kids on the second and fourth weekend or you'll never have a free weekend together.

They chattered, directing the discussion at us, and I felt unusually desirable. They were each trying to have a little conversation with one of us, or trying to get noticed by one of us. The chatter was fast and funny, and once again, it was therapeutic to have pretty women not treat me like a child molester as my ex-wife had once falsely accused me of being. At that moment, I thought that I could not ask for more than a life of pleasant conversations like this.

An hour later, my friend and I excused ourselves to go to the men's room and when we came back, the women had all rearranged themselves, so we were sitting beside different people.

Alicia

Alicia, one of the ladies at the Southport Brewery that night, was the only one I really sparked with. I went to her house the next Saturday afternoon. She lived beside the Belmont Golf Course, and it had just snowed. Her three girls were with their dad that weekend (an "A" weekend), so we had the house to ourselves. I never did meet the girls, not that I wanted to. I came to understand that moms protect their kids, and an introduction to a new man is a big moment, potentially threatening to all parties.

The first date is always the most exciting.

It was sunny and cold. We took the sleds down the back porch and joined up with a group of neighbors who were sledding. I was introduced, but it was a loose group, and we were soon by ourselves. There were good vibes between us, and most of the time I was just enjoying the moment. But a couple times I wondered what we might do after the fun in the snow, since this was an evening date also. The house was warm and inviting, and the vibes I was getting were all inviting.

At the bottom of the hill one time, Alicia ended up upside down in the snow beside me and she looked over and kissed me on the lips. Quick. Friendly. Invitingly. Not passionately. But nice.

Whoa! A milestone! I hadn't touched the first woman I dated. I hugged the second. And got a smooch from the third. It kept getting better! I guess I never thought about how exciting a new relationship could be: the uncertainty, the possibilities, the newness.

We went back to the house and pulled simple food out of the fridge: a barbequed chicken, some mayo, and bread. She opened a window and reached for a pack of slim cigarettes from the top shelf of a cabinet, an apologetic look in her eyes. "Do you mind?" I pulled a pack from my coat, and we both had a little laugh and then a smoke.

She poured us each a large snifter of Jack Daniels and in the early evening light we each quickly had a buzz.

In the next hour, four things happened in quick succession. Alicia and I held and rocked each other on the couch. I completely melted, and she was probably surprised or confused when I quietly cried. The feeling of her acceptance touched right through my armor to my sorrow. She responded by closing her eyes and rocking me harder, like quieting a crying infant. Then my ex called on my cell to yell at me for not calling the kids that evening. The mood was broken, my composure regained, and the armor back in place.

I simply turned the cell off and smiled at Alicia. Then, as we walked back to the kitchen and passed the front door, I asked if she wanted me to turn the lock. She said she never locked the front door because her ex sometimes dropped over unexpectedly. I tried to wrestle with that vision, but simply could not. Then she switched subjects and explained that she was a teacher's assistant, and her alimony stopped in eighteen months. Why would she say that on a first date? My psyche was not too stable when I got there that day, but to think I could handle those four inputs in such rapid succession was too much.

We kissed a bit, that first-time kissing when you are exploring each other's personality and reactions. There is a smirk on my face now as I write this; I couldn't believe the success I was having. We had another Jack Daniels and a couple more smokes, and I drove home, thinking about the complexities. My dreams that night had red flags waving everywhere, above me, on billboards, flying behind airplanes, and tied to trees. But I called her the next day, and we went out four or five more times.

Probably the turning point was talking to her on the phone one night, and every time one of her kids asked her a question, she put down the phone for minutes at a time. I was too needy and selfish to find this attractive. And when I had a choice, I called someone else.

Givers, Takers, and Dating

I asked another woman out to dinner during one of our first phone chats. She agreed to meet me at a restaurant in Belmont. I got there early and got a table in the back and struck up a conversation with the waitress. It was slow that night, and so we talked on and off for half an hour. She was a cute woman with a British accent, an athletic body, full lips, and a great smile. From her standing position beside my table, she could see the front door. She reported to me on everyone who walked in and speculated whether each could be the unseen date.

"This one's looking for someone," my British waitress friend said.

I caught sight of the approaching woman in the mirror on the far wall. "If she's 160 pounds like her online profile says, I'll eat my hat."

The waitress friend chuckled and walked away, and the date walked over. We exchanged introductions and sat down for dinner. She was not unattractive in the face and body, and as I drank a second and then a third glass of wine, she got downright good looking. She did most of the talking. She said that as a divorce attorney (!), she didn't have much time for social meetings like this. She was not a happy person. We parted shortly after dinner, and I later wrote her a thanks-but-no-thanks email to which she responded angrily.

Lesson learned: don't commit to an expensive dinner until you have met.

One thing about online dating is that everybody lies. The women lie about their weight. The men lie about their age, and even the online dating service lies—about how many miles it is to the person you are winking at. This understanding came to me on a dark weekday night as I drove forty-eight miles down the interstate to a rendezvous at Borders with a short woman who the online dating service said was "under twenty-five miles" from my location. Maybe as the crow flies or in a time warp. Who knows?

I was done suffering through dinners with ugly or angry people. If she's not simpatico, you have to be able to get out after a few minutes. This person was not attractive. All the way home down the interstate, I had plenty of time to rearrange my approach. *Like no more dates without a picture first,* I thought. I sent her an email when I got home and got another angry email in response. She didn't like it that I had traded IMs with her for a week before meeting because she thought there was something of a relationship implied in that. Oh, brother.

I felt myself getting colder, less sympathetic, more selfish. I thought this to myself and was okay with the thought. I rationalized that I had spent my entire adult life giving, and now I was going to get a little balance back in my life (translation: I was going to give less and take more). This is a position that I would debate with myself many times in the coming years. I wanted the companionship of a good woman and had less and less patience with those who didn't spark with me. I would work on improving my filter.

Maybe I was not colder. Maybe people in this life, in general, are either givers or takers. The intensity of this attribute in a person may change, and few people are either totally one or totally the other. My mother says I am a giver. She had six children and is a giver herself. In the interest of balance and mental health, a giver has to know boundaries and be able to prevent takers from taking too much, even if you love the takers. This is a fine line that few people perfect. I had not.

Take a moment and think about givers, takers, and dating. Takers will gravitate to givers and vice versa. Can an overly giving parent produce, by his excessive giving, a taking child, thereby harming the child? This question brings up another question: Are givers inherently good and takers inherently bad?

Indeed, I hypothesize that most entrepreneurs, as well as having undiagnosed ADHD, are also high on the "takers" scale. A person has to be focused enough to push a project through, despite all the detractors and obstacles. So, economies and jobs and bread on the table come from takers.

Equally, I would hypothesize that mothers and teachers are high on the "givers" scale.

Since traditionally men have been the breadwinners and women have been the teachers, does "givers and takers" have gender associations as well? A couple fairly simple experiments would confirm or deny these hypotheses.

If we assume that a person can move up and down the "givers and takers" scale, the next question is, what factors can induce that movement? Is the prospect of old age a factor, similar to the supposition that people are more anarchistic and Democratic in their early adulthood, and more Republican in their older age?

Since I introduced the hypothesis above that most entrepreneurs have undiagnosed ADHD, let's expand on that and ask if particular medical conditions appear more in givers than in takers. Further, are givers attracted to the Democratic Party and takers attracted to the Republican Party? Does your circle of friends influence your givers or takers position? Does the situation influence you to modify your thoughts or actions in this regard? If you are with just one person, is it easier to be a giver than if you are in a group or crowd?

Can you consciously move yourself along the spectrum? In the eight years since my divorce, I have consciously felt myself becoming less giving and far more taking. That, I think, comes from a feeling that I was being taken advantage of, from a realization that my support network was actually less supportive than I had thought ten years ago, and from other factors I cannot separate at this point in my development. And I recognize that doing so much for others weakened both them and me. Sometimes the balance is hard to find. I am enjoying life more now because of my divorce (and because of many other factors), but I also have had more bottom-of-the-well sorrow recently, as some people in my life have moved away, partially, I believe, because they do not understand the change in me that subtle movements along the givers and takers continuum has produced.

Enough thinking. Back to feeling. Which brings us to ...

Liz

Liz was enjoyable to be around. The Parents without Partners lead lady called me a few weeks after the restaurant meeting with the six women to see if I was still available because she had a good friend who was very classy and had broken up with her boyfriend. She called to see if I was interested.

Liz turned out to be *very* classy, and we had a lot in common. It was an easy friendship. We met for lunch the first time, and then for dinner and a play. Her old boyfriend was still on her mind, but other than that, she was good company: a good conversationalist who knew how to talk and how to listen. For the play she wore a stunning little black dress. She was 5 foot 6, with shoulder-length auburn hair, just the right amount of lipstick, artsy earrings, high heels, and as she walked away, a wiggle that gets men's attention.

That was the night for one of life's little embarrassing moments that you never forget but wish you could. I did not end up in bed with any of these women. Not even close. But I never wanted to eliminate the possibility, so I carried protection in my jacket pocket beside my wallet. And sure enough, that night in the restaurant before the play, as I pulled out my wallet to pay the bill, that little plastic package jumped right onto the middle of the table. We each looked at it, I quickly made it disappear, and she excused herself to go to the ladies' room, probably to spare my feelings while she laughed herself silly.

We still see each other from time to time at the friend's house. Life is funny.

Mary

My neighbor, Katerina, hooked me up with a friend of hers, Mary. I found a friend for Katerina, and we all double-dated at the Blues Café. Mary and I left early to get out of the noise and to have a cigarette. We went to the Rusty Scupper, where we sat at the bar and exchanged life stories. I started to appreciate how gentle and pretty Mary was. But there was no spark. Katerina and my friend joined us a couple hours later. Evidently no spark there either.

My good friend and neighbor Mookie never met Alicia, Liz, Christine, Mary, or Trish. She did meet Carol.

Carol

Carol and I met through MatchMaker.com. The first date, after a couple weeks of messaging and phone calls, was a late-summer evening tailgate picnic at a state park by the ocean. I brought wine and cheese, she brought crackers and a salad. We sat there leaning against the minivan's open back. We didn't notice the sun going down and the parking lot lights coming on. She was a very accepting and gentle woman, a schoolteacher. She had no animosity or ill feelings about anyone, including her cheating ex. She was passionate (about her kids, and other things), but thankfully not intense. That was so refreshing for me.

When the bottle of wine was empty, I realized it was dark, and as I turned my head toward her, I noticed she was staring at me. We kissed. A long, hungry kiss, it kept going on and on. Neither of us knew what to do with our hands, so they sort of hung there at our sides, like teenagers' hands. I so welcomed her accepting and gentle spirit. The spark between us was gentle.

We dated exclusively for four months at the end of 2002. We went to several movies and restaurants, and shared one weekend away in Boston. She was genuine. And soft. Carol was a tall, slender, and attractive redhead with an easy laugh. We had so many things in common; it was an easy fit. Her third child was still at home, and I was introduced. In fact, he was one of the few kids I ever met. He was at home doing homework or in front of the TV several evenings when we were on the back porch talking.

Carol was a survivor. Not a warrior, but a survivor. She was too nice and forgiving, and kept getting hurt. She shared several stories about her students and took me to a school play one dark, rainy, autumn evening. She was fun to be with and accepting, which was a big ingredient that I craved.

But in the final analysis, I was attracted by magic more than by comfort, and I came to realize that my heart had found that magic in my neighbor. I could not erase the memories of Katerina, or the hope. I had to leave Carol to try to get Katerina. That breakup was horrible. But my mantra in these years was to keep moving. And I took comfort in my mantra, and I hid behind it. I almost said to myself that it was okay to break Carol's heart and traumatize her because I needed to keep moving.

Dear reader, you have to decide this one for yourself. I can give you a dozen good reasons why leaving was the right thing to do, and a dozen reasons why I should not have caused the pain. But I did it because I had to.

Katerina

Because I was in love with Katerina. Magic Katerina. So many moments, firsts, new experiences—an altitude halfway to Saturn. One story will have to suffice for now. Just before Christmas 2002, I had been dating Carol. I had just returned home after work and then grocery shopping. Molly, my dog, was just inside the door of #218, waiting to be walked after nine hours alone. I approached my door, 25-pound bag of dog food under one arm, keys and laptop in the other. Katerina came down the hall, heading to Mookie's door opposite mine.

The tall vision was wearing a black jumpsuit, lace at the shoulders, butt and breasts well-presented like she owned the world. Her silky hair was pulled back and up, showing her Audrey Hepburn neck. Three-inch heels made her taller than I am. She smiled at me and said offhandedly that she was going to a Christmas party. She knocked on Mookie's door and vanished inside. I realized the sack of dog food had fallen onto the floor and my jaw onto my chest. That vision will never, ever, leave my brain.

That evening was really the end of this chapter in my life, although I did not realize it then.

Dating and Why HIPAA Is a Good Idea

Good luck is opportunity meeting preparedness.
—Deepak Chopra

Just after the divorce, during my initial attempts to get back into the dating scene, I realized that it was sometimes a challenge to get my body to participate in the good times. So, on the next trip to the doctor, I convinced him to let me try the little blue pill that I had heard so much about. All that I will say about its effectiveness, for me anyway, is that its advertising claims are not overstated.

One day I was at the pharmacy getting a refill, because they only put six pills at a time in each prescription.

Why only six? **You probably don't need thirty**; it's not something most guys take every day. Should they put in four, one for each weekend for a month? One a week or two a week for a month? For a semester? No, probably college guys don't need this. Or maybe they *do* want this for an extra boost or for bragging rights? How do doctors figure out how many should be in a prescription? Or is that an individual doctor's decision? Did my doctor look at his pathetic middle-aged patient and think to himself, "Six is more than he'll ever need"?

And guess what? I tried cutting one in half when I only had one left, and it worked the same as the whole one. What's with that? Was I overdosing the earlier times? Can you really overdose on this stuff? What would happen? Would you die from lack of blood to the brain or heart? What would the EMTs say when they found you? Maybe, "Bro, this dude overdosed. Man! I wish I could do that without dying!"

And have you ever wondered, compared to the $12 pill, how effective all those cheap imitations advertised in the back of *Popular Science* magazine are? (And why did they choose *that* magazine to congregate in? Like all us techies have unfulfilled libidos?) Are there different chemicals in those, or are they just made in Beijing instead of in Indianapolis? Or do they just not use exact scales, so you may get 0.8X or 1.2X instead of 1.0X +/− 0.05? What's the difference? And if the FDA has not approved it, why does the FDA allow it to be advertised in a national magazine and allow it to be bought and taken? And if I take it, will it have the same effect? Too many questions!

So anyway, I went to get my first refill at the pharmacy in a part of town known for its geriatric demographics. This was in 2003, at a time before HIPAA. The pharmacist was required, as they are now, to make sure that she or he was giving the right medicine to the right patient, but back then the pharmacist would speak your name and the drug name out loud as a safety check to make sure the prescription was yours and didn't belong to the guy waiting patiently over on the plastic lawn chair. And the pharmacist would ask if you wanted any instructions about taking the medication.

One time I contemplated what the pharmacist would say if I asked for instructions. But I didn't feel like a provocateur that day and didn't. On this particular day, the pharmacist was slow and as she was getting my pills, a line of middle-aged and elderly women formed behind me. I turned at one point, a bit self-conscious, to see if there was anyone I knew, and sure enough, there was a friend of the ex, three people back. We exchanged suspicious nods of acknowledgment and I turned back toward the counter just as the pharmacist called out, in a voice like the drill sergeant used when addressing the whole squad, "Kenly? Viagra!"

So now the whole store knew that I was experiencing some ED, or maybe that I was trying to impress the girls. Either way, it was TMI! I sighed as I signed my name in the pharmacist's logbook, feeling that the blush had reached my face and my big ears. I took my bag and mentally prepared to turn and walk the gauntlet, past these pre- and post-menopausal women, each of whom were enjoying their own comic mental scene that, I was sure in my own egocentric way, featured me. Surely the ex would hear about this before the end of the day!

I could either slink out, or go out with style, I thought. And since I've never been much into slinking, I just turned and smiled and proclaimed as I held the prescription bag high, *"Somebody's going to be happy tonight!"*

I can be such a jerk sometimes.

Dating after Divorce

Even Love Sometimes Must Scratch Its Head & Wonder

People

Underestimate love,

Religiously we blunder.

Even love sometimes must scratch its head & wonder.

If by chance with

Nothing better to do in the interim

How can it comfort us & mentor them?

Establish trust and center them?

A love that has no limits is limitless indeed

Religiously love should be all we ever need

Too often its seeds we cast asunder …

… Even love sometimes must scratch its head & wonder.

—Tony Haynes

Chapter 10

Dating After Divorce: Stories and a Few Little Extra Anecdotes

The Crazy Psychiatrist

Barbie called and told me she had decided it was time I started dating, and she had found this fabulous man for me. He is very well known, a published and respected psychiatrist. He also owns several facilities in multiple states. She asked me if she could give him my number, and I said, "Sure, what do I have to lose?" He called me, and we ended up talking on the phone for a couple of weeks. He seemed pleasant, so I decided to join him for lunch.

Every time we tried to make plans, things came up that were acts of God, and we had to keep rescheduling. I should have noticed those acts of God and recognized them as possible GodWinks trying to tell me, "Don't go, dear! Run, run very fast in the other direction." I did not follow my GodWinks and eventually went on the lunch date. Oh Lord, one day I will learn to listen to you better! (For more on GodWinks, please see the first book in this series: *Divorced and Scared No More: Emotional Support for the Newly Divorced.*)

When I first arrived, everything seemed very reasonable. He was a bit shorter and older than I was, but that was not a big problem. As we talked, I noticed he was a brilliant man. I could tell every question he asked was asked for a reason. I can think, chat, and eat all at the same time, so once again, no problem. You can ask anyone who knows me; I am very rarely at a loss for words. His questions started to become more and more intrusive, so I decided to turn the tables on him and ask him about personal issues as well. He is like many other men who love to talk about themselves and all of their accomplishments. During our lunch date, I learned a lot about serial killers. As well as some of the famous patients he had written about in his books.

The subject eventually turned to his ex-wives and the subsequent divorces, including the fights, even the one that involved frozen embryos. At that point, he said he could understand why serial killers do what they do and how they justify their actions logically. At that point, I knew I needed to eat faster and get out of that restaurant. As the waiter refilled my water glass, out of nowhere, the crazy psychiatrist asked me if I would marry him, and if I did, he offered to pay me a large amount of money. He stated he liked my mind and the fact that I could process thoughts while I talked and was fully aware of my surroundings. He needed a partner who would accompany him to social functions and be able to keep him informed of everything going on. The waiter almost spilled water all over the table, while I nearly choked on my food.

I told him I was not currently interested or looking for marriage, and now would be a good time to end this lunch date. He seemed to get very agitated with my response and asked that I stay awhile as he ate dessert. I was starting to wonder if I was sitting next to Hannibal Lecter. When dessert came, he was upset the waiter did not bring two forks. I couldn't believe he thought I would share dessert with him! That was the last straw. I thanked him for lunch and got up to leave. He grabbed my hand and asked when we could have another date, to which my response was, "I don't think that would be possible."

A few days later, he started calling and pleading for another date. He then offered to help my cousin's wife get leads for a job. She is a counselor, and he even offered to meet with her and give her pointers, plus personal recommendations. I told her about my experience with him, but since jobs were hard to find in those days, she wanted to meet with him. When she arrived, she found him dressed in a sweat-suit with a suit on top. None of his leads ever turned out to be at all helpful. She was disappointed—but back to the story. He continued to call me, and I sent his calls straight to voicemail. Thank goodness for voicemail!

Six months later, I purchased a new phone, and unfortunately, my phone numbers did not transfer well into my new phone's address book. Much of my contact information was lost. The psychiatrist's phone number had been on the go-straight-to-voicemail list, but when the contact information was lost, the filter no longer worked.

One day my phone rang, and I did not know the number, so I answered, and discovering it was the crazy psychiatrist, I quickly excused myself and hung up the phone. Then he started calling multiple times a day, and with every voicemail he left, he became angrier.

One day I was in Arkansas at a family reunion at my cousin's house, and I once again answered a call without knowing who was on the end of the line. The psychiatrist had stopped using his cell, which was back on the straight-to-voicemail list, and had begun using other phones to call me. Due to the expression on my face, my cousin's husband asked me who was on the phone. I replied, "the crazy psychiatrist." Then I looked down at the phone and realized I had not hung up the phone. At first, I was worried about his reaction to hearing me calling him "the crazy psychiatrist" due to his escalation (using different phones to call me). Fortunately for me, I have never heard from this man again.

I finally decided to call Barbie and tell her how odd he was. She said he was a friend of her husband's, and she would talk to him. A couple of days later, she called and admitted her husband only knew him through a friend. The moral to this story is: If your friend is setting you up on a blind date, make sure they know the other person. This horrible date was the reason I started contacting restaurants ahead of time to arrange safety phrases.

Private Security Contractor

When I am working on something, I become extremely focused on the task at hand, and I do not pay much attention to the things going on around me. Yes, it also includes times when I am doing my volunteer work. Meeting someone to date is the farthest thing from my mind.

One day, at the local community center, I was helping the center get ready for a party for underprivileged children. While trying to decorate the room, I literally ran into a gentleman who was trying to help. We both dropped everything all over the floor. As I was apologizing for my gracefulness and trying to pick everything up, he commented, "I always notice when a redhead walks into the room. They are blondes on fire!" What an opening statement to say to a redhead! I had to look up to see who this man was with such a great sense of humor. Without missing a beat, I responded, "You didn't notice me too well if you ran into me."

From that moment on, we texted, called daily, and met for coffee a few times. Thank goodness I did stick to my rule of not revealing my last name or address until I feel very comfortable with a person. Glenn and I seemed to click from the first moment. He was one of those people who could make me laugh, and I love laughter. I noticed his schedule was so flexible. I finally asked what he did for a living. He told me he was a private security contractor, and I knew that meant a mercenary because two of my cousins had been in the military's Special Forces. I thought, "Oh well, what the heck. That is just a job, and I should accept him as a private citizen."

Things got interesting when Glenn was called to go overseas on a mission. This nice, stable man, all of a sudden, started asking me to send him photographs of where I was. He even asked me at 2 a.m. to send him a photo of my bedroom. I received many text messages each day, asking me who I was with and what I was doing. After about a week, I started becoming very uncomfortable with his behavior. I emailed him about how I was feeling and said that when he got back home, maybe we could talk again. But until then, while he was overseas, it would be best for him to keep focused on his task at hand.

He became agitated and told me, "I know you work out at the gym four or more days a week. There are only three in your town and seven within driving distance of your city. I have photographs of what you look like, and I can have somebody following you within a very very short time." When anyone threatens me, I have one of two options: cower in fear or come back strong. I usually choose the latter, whether I feel it or not, and my Dad taught me how to play poker very well. Thus, my response to him was, "Assuming I was like most girls was a big mistake. As you know, I have a concealed handgun license and carry a gun with me. If anyone tries to hurt me, I will not hesitate to protect myself."

Honestly, I was not that good at keeping my gun with me. Often, I left it home, but from that moment on, I decided keeping it with me was a necessity. That day, I had the company that monitors the security system on my property come over to make sure there were no holes in my system that someone could get through.

One day at the gym, my friend Ryan noticed I was carrying my bag with me from machine to machine. He came up and said, "CHL?" and I said, "Yeah, how do you know?" He said, "Most of us who carry a bag with us in the gym, probably have the same thing you're carrying in our bags as well." I shared with him what Glenn had said, and he looked at me with a smile and said, "Don't worry T, you're always safe here." He asked to see a photograph of Glenn, which he, in turn, shared with some of our other friends at the gym. Upon Glenn's arrival back stateside, he called to apologize and told me that many wives and girlfriends cheat on their spouses or boyfriends when men are in the field overseas. He then asked if we could go out for coffee and start over. I told him that I did not think that was such a good idea and wished him well. I cannot be involved in any relationship where someone is trying to control or threaten me. They have no place in my life. Domestic violence is rarely an isolated incident. Instead, it is a pattern of behavior aimed at establishing and maintaining power and control over someone. That is why it is one of my deal-breakers.

The pattern is typically described as a cycle of violence because the abuser is not always cruel. Since the seriousness and effects of abuse escalate in each subsequent cycle, the pattern of domestic violence can also be described as a spiral. At its worst, the spiral can end in the death of the victim. You can read more about the cycle of violence and its warning signs in *Divorced and Scared No More: Emotional Support for the Newly Divorced.*

If you or someone you know needs further information on this topic, please go to domesticviolence.org, or contact the National Domestic Violence Hotline at 1-800-799-7233 (SAFE). If you are outside of the U.S., please search on the internet to find some assistance near you.

Don't Skip Dating Rules

Due to a very hectic schedule, I wasn't able to make my typical preparations for a first date. My date was a successful businessman, and we were to meet at a lovely restaurant in Midtown. I thought, *What the heck. I can skip a few of my dating rules.* I know what you are thinking: famous last words. And you were right.

We sat at a table in the middle of the room. After I sat down, I noticed he looked very different from his picture. There was just something about his sideburns. I looked more closely, and I realized what it was: He dyed his hair black and had a line across his sideburns; below the line, his sideburns were pure white. I couldn't help it—I kept looking at them and thinking to myself, *why doesn't somebody tell this man to comb the dye through the sideburns for the last five or ten minutes to give a salt-and-pepper look?*

The food was terrific, but I started noticing the waiter never asked if I wanted another glass of wine. There was always a fresh full glass of wine right next to my plate. At that point, I started drinking more of my water. My date had been trying to tell me what to order, and finally, I told him I do not like the type of seafood he wanted me to order. Eventually, he gave in and decided I did not have to order the oysters.

This restaurant serves cotton candy with a sparkler in it for birthdays. Whenever someone gets it, the entire restaurant turns to looks at the person. The lady behind me was receiving her cotton candy, and at the same time, my date felt it was appropriate to start feeding me the oysters to convince me that I would like them—using the fork he had just used to take his first few bites.

With the whole restaurant looking at the lady behind me, I didn't want to make a scene, so I took the bite, and he continued trying to feed me more. I was extremely uncomfortable in part because I have a thing about my face and mouth after having it rebuilt so many times since I was in a car accident. Additionally, I am a grown woman and very capable of feeding myself; I have done this little task for most of my life.

A few moments later, he motioned for me to come closer. Since the restaurant was loud, I thought he was going to tell me something. Oh no—he started kissing me right there in front of everybody! After what he'd just done, the man thought it was appropriate to ask me to go to his place to see the view of the city lights. Of course, my answer was, "No, I have just moved from Vegas and have seen lots of pretty lights." If he would do all of that on a first date in a restaurant full of people, what would this man do if he got someone alone

I usually do not use valet parking, but I think it is best to splurge and stay in the safety of the restaurant when on your first few dates with anyone, especially if, as in this case, the non-valet parking for the restaurant is a block or two away. As we headed out to the valet parking, my date turned and asked, "There's not going to be a story about me on your website, is there?" I looked at him, smiled, and then said, "What would I have to write about you?" The valet arrived, and I waved goodbye, got in my car, and drove home, where I promptly put his phone number on the straight-to-voicemail list.

Not All Cross-dressers Are the Same

While checking my online dating site, I received a wink and an email. I clicked to see the profile of the gentleman who sent the wink and the message, and the main photo appeared to show an attractive woman. I am an inquisitive person and just had to see what was going on. The first thing I read was that this gentleman was a cross-dresser.

Reading the rest of his profile, he seemed to be a very nice Christian man who just happened to like to wear women's clothes. I emailed him to say thank you for the wink and the very kind words. I ended the email by explaining to him that I didn't think we would be a good match and wishing him good luck with his search. His response back to me said, "I understand, I get that a lot. I haven't had a date in over four years." That touched my heart. I felt compelled to tell this nice man that he needed to overhaul his approach to improve his chances of finding the right woman.

He was a handsome man, and the words in his profile were great. I suggested he tweak his profile a bit and maybe he would have better luck getting dates. We live in one of the biggest cities in the United States, and there had to be someone out there just for him.

That was the beginning of our adventure in revising his profile. We looked at everything, section by section. He wanted to be upfront with women about his clothing choices, but in the past, there had been women who responded to his lifestyle by using very hurtful words that still hurt him very deeply. I advised him to change his main profile photo to one where he was not in a dress but a suit instead. Oh my, what a handsome man he is. That photo was sure to get any woman's attention.

Every day I would get an email that said, "T, I am just not sure about this; I want to be truthful." I would respond, telling him, "It is admirable that you want to be truthful, but we need to package you a little differently. Everyone has something in his or her closet (no pun intended), and it is great that you want them to know before any communication. You have a lot to offer, so let them see that first! Cross-dressing is only a part of who you are. Think of the dating site as a place you are advertising yourself. Sell yourself and then say something like, 'Oh, by the way, I also like wearing dresses. We can go shopping together, and I can give you advice on what looks good on you.'"

Day by day, the dress photo was moved back on his pictures until it was the last of his eight. Also, his paragraph about cross-dressing and how he felt about it was moved to the end. His profile now ended with, "Don't worry ladies, I won't ask to share any of your clothes if you don't ask to share any of mine. LOL."

About a week after the new profile was posted, he sent me an email telling me he had gotten more winks and emails in that one week than he had in a whole year. Then the big news came: He had a date that night! I was so happy for him! I had to ask, "You are not wearing a dress tonight, right?" His response was, "No, it isn't a dress night! T, you're right about cross-dressing. That it is not the most important part of who I am; it is only one part of who I am. My date tonight does know about my wardrobe choices and seems to understand. I should not let those insensitive, cruel women of my past ruin my future!" As of this writing, they have been together, dating exclusively and happily, for over year.

I am back out in the dating-to-get-to-know-people world again, and I have to share this recent story. I met this man, and one evening he called and asked what I wanted the dating to evolve into within the next few months. I responded that eventually, I would like to find a committed relationship with someone. He then told me he was working, and the conversation needed to continue via texting.

The text I received stated that he would like to have a relationship that would lead to marriage, and he would be monogamous but did *not* want his wife to be. I texted back, "Did I read that correctly?" and he replied, "Yes" with a photo attached of him in a red dress. I called my friend Jill and told her about the latest installment of the "soap opera I call life" and then I found out she knows the man. What a small big city Houston is. I also found out from another friend that the crazy psychiatrist is now dating a man who dresses up in women's dresses. I wonder if it is the guy with the red dress.

Lake Party

The Fourth of July was coming, and Rick, a good friend from high school, called to ask if I'd like to go with him to a party and see an old friend for a potluck dinner at his house on the lake. Rick was told there would be an artist there to paint artwork on our bodies. We thought that might be kind of fun. We had not seen Matt since high school, and that was over twenty years ago. I remembered our friend Matt being a tall, handsome, and conservative person. With our dish to pass in hand, and swimsuits just in case there might be a dip in the lake on this hot summer day, we headed to the party.

Rick and I lived in the city, and it took about an hour to get to the lake. The drive seemed short because we had plenty of catching up to do. When we arrived, most of the people were sitting outside in the front yard. The potluck went fabulously, with lots of interesting and delicious food and an eclectic group of people. We sat down and watched a beautiful sunset together. As I turned and looked back at the group, I noticed the look on their faces. It was like they were speaking to each other without saying a word. As if something was about to happen, and Rick and I were the only two who didn't know what it was. I shook the feeling off, thinking I was just being silly. What could happen?

Soon it was my turn to get my fake tattoo. I'm afraid to get a real tattoo, on anything other than permanent makeup, because I've heard they hurt. While working on my tattoo, the artist looked at us and said, "The two of you don't seem to fit in with this group. How well do you know these people?" Then I heard a lady behind me say, "Can you make my nipple the center of the flower?" Rick reached down and grabbed my arm. I looked up at him, and then I looked over at her. Yep, her top was off, and she was planning to get her entire chest painted in flowers. I turned to look at Rick, and we now shared a look that said, "How the heck do we get out of here, and what kind of party are we at?" He grabbed my arm tighter. I turned and looked around again and saw there were four more women with their tops off. Soon I would be the only woman with anything other than a bathing suit bottom on her body.

I had no problem in high school saying "No" and I have no problem now, so my shirt stayed on. Rick and I tried to act like nothing unusual was happening, although we were trying to figure out how quickly we could get out of this place. We didn't know what they had planned next and didn't want to find out. All of a sudden, the host said, "Time to go swimming!" Even though we had our suits in the car, we were not wearing them. So, we thanked them and said, "Sorry, we can't because we don't have any swimsuits." Matt then told us, "Neither do we. There are no swimsuits on this moonlight dip!" Rick had just texted me a few minutes before, so I knew my cell phone screen was on that text. I reached in my bag and rubbed my fingers on the screen. Luckily, the phone sent the gibberish text. As Rick looked down at the text, he told Matt we had to get back to town because there was a problem he had to attend to immediately. We collected our things as they headed to the beach, waving goodbye with smiles and thanking Matt for inviting us. Needless to say, we weren't giving goodbye hugs. Quickly we got into the car and started the drive back. It was about a quarter of a mile before either of us would even look at each other. When we finally did, we burst out laughing. Neither of us could believe how much our high school friend had changed. Then Rick decided to ask me if I would take off my top and show him my boobies, just so he could compare, to which my response was a whack upside his head.

It is nice being out with a person who is just a good old friend!

Texting Freddy and Eddy

Social networks, emailing, and texting has become a significant focus of our everyday lives. They are also tools we use within our dating world. I do not allow anyone I am dating to be a "friend" of mine on my social network. For more tips on good practices for social media usage after divorce, please see *Divorced and Scared No More: Practical Advice for the Newly Divorced.*

As I wrote about earlier in this book, I have a filtering process for online dating. Emailing is the first phase; the next is texting, then talking on the phone, the meet and greet, and then finally the date. Most of the time, this has worked very well, and my dates are reserved for people with whom I share similar interests.

I met Freddy and Eddy at about the same time on an online dating site. It's just my luck that I have dyslexia, and I was communicating with two people with similar names. Even so, I was doing very well, keeping things relatively straight regarding who I was texting and who I was emailing. Before I go on the first date, I always make sure that it's very obvious things will progress slowly, and we will take our time getting to know one another.

Freddy's job required extensive travel, and he was out of town often. Whenever we went out, it was always to take part in a very fun-filled activity. Eddy is a widower from an affluent family in the city; definitely, a man used to getting his way. On our second date, Eddy informed me that he would like to plan some family activities for both of our families to get to know each other. I expressed that I did not feel it was appropriate to include my family at this point in dating.

While driving home after the date, I was trying to decide if I wanted to see Eddy again. I looked in my rearview mirror, and I saw Eddy's very distinctive vehicle approximately two cars behind me. Immediately I drove to the nearest police station, pulled into the parking lot and watched his vehicle drive off. Putting it mildly, I was furious. When I arrived home, I decided to text him. All the text said was, "I don't think this relationship will work out. Good luck in your search!" Then Freddy texted me back saying, "Sorry to hear that T. If you change your mind, you have my number."

Yep, I texted the wrong man. So, remember, once the word is spoken or the text message is sent, it is not easily explained or taken it back. I wasn't brave enough at the time to tell Freddy what had happened.

You've Been Married How Many Times?

We all know that some people stretch or embellish the truth when meeting a new person for a potential romantic relationship. Jonathan is a few years younger than I am and lives in my neighborhood. We have many things in common; for example, we both love fishing and sailing. Often on his way home from work, he will text message me to meet him at the lake with the fishing stuff and a couple of beers. It is nice to take in the wonderful outdoors and share the events of the day.

On one enlightening afternoon, Jonathan started telling me about the eight times he has been married. He shared with me that his last marriage was to a woman who would literally growl like a dog every time he or his friends mentioned going sailing. I couldn't help myself, and I had to ask, "How long do you wait to start dating again after you end a relationship?" Jonathan said, "Oh, usually by the next Friday or Saturday because you know when it is over." At that point, I decided Jonathan would remain as my fishing buddy, but nothing more.

On another occasion, some of my friends planned on going out to shoot some pool the next Friday. I asked Jonathan if he would like to go with us. He said, "I'd love to, but I have a date." I could not help it; I looked over at him and said, "Is she in the running for the number nine spot?" He replied, "Yes, because I do not believe in having sex outside of marriage." That may have something to do with why he married so many times.

Having a fulfilling sex life is vital for most people, but being able to justify having sex with a particular person is not a good reason for marriage. Too bad Jonathan doesn't see that taking his time to find the right person with whom he has the potential of sharing a lasting relationship is more important.

Some are just looking for a good time, and that is fine. Others are looking for a long-term relationship with or without marriage, and once again, that is also fine. Then there are people looking to find someone just so they can get married because they do not want to be alone, but they do not understand marriage or the vows that are taken for the real reason of joining two people in holy matrimony.

Make sure you are clear about what you want, and what your intentions are when you are getting involved with someone. By taking it slow, you can learn what the other person has in mind, and this is the best way to avoid a costly heart-breaking mistake.

Always Ask If There Is Something about Them You Need to Know

Going to the gym not only will make you feel better and look better but also most of the time, you will also have a good view. One day I noticed a gentleman who was the appropriate age for me, about 6 feet 3 inches tall, handsome, and very physically fit. Our workout schedules seemed to coincide. One day, I was trying to adjust a weight machine, but it seemed to be stuck. I can be a little on the stubborn side, and I wasn't going to let this machine get the better of me. I started trying to pull the thing to adjust it. All of a sudden, it let loose, and everything came flying down on my thumb. As I sat there in pain, hoping no one had noticed, I heard a deep French voice behind me saying, "Put your thumb in here, it will help." Keith had gotten a cup of ice for me to put my purple thumb in to relieve some of the pain and reduce swelling.

We began talking every time we saw each other at the gym. It was nice to have someone to work out with and hold me accountable for showing up. While working out, we would share some of our dating stories and laugh. I usually only have a date or two with most men and then move on because, I don't know about you, but I can tell within about five or ten minutes if there is chemistry or not. Even though dating doesn't always work out, I have made several good guy friends. Keith didn't see it that way. He accused me of being a serial dater, and I said, "I'm not a serial dater. I'm just picky. Why waste both of our time if I am not interested? You can't make yourself have feelings if they are not there."

Several times he asked if I would like to go to the park for a picnic after our workout. The park may be public, but it isn't like a restaurant, coffee house, or the gym. Parks and beaches are not an option for me until I know a person very well. Eventually, I looked at him and asked, "Is there anything about you that makes you unique or that I might need to know?" That's when he told me that he is a nudist, which surprised me. Without missing a beat, I invited him to come to my church and maybe my Christian Singles Group, but that we should keep the nudist stuff quiet. I think nudity trumps perspicacious dating.

We have remained friends, work out together, email, and give each other advice on the opposite sex, but we don't date. Keith knows that for me, clothes are not optional; they are required. I can't date a man who likes to show everything to everyone. Besides, I like my clothes and enjoy picking out what I am going to wear. They keep me warm on a cold winter's day, and they hide all those little flaws that I only allow a special someone to see.

Am I Too Picky?

While starting my website, I decided to contact some friends who know about computers and how websites are built. At the time of my divorce, I knew how to turn the computer on, turn it off, how to use email, and occasionally shop.

I met Ray through a friend because there was a specific talent he had with computers. He quickly saw I have no clue about networks other than the basics. Ray asked me out, and I agreed to meet him for lunch. Even though he was an acquaintance, I still chose to go to one of the restaurants that I use for first dates. I called them in the evening and let them know I would be there the next day. A particularly favorite of mine is a very nice restaurant in Midtown, and Robert is my waiter who always takes care of me.

It was nice to have the opportunity to talk about things other than computers, and the date seemed to be going very well. Then all of a sudden, he reached up, put his finger in his nose, picked his nose, and then ate it. Every time he talked to me from that point on, I noticed he would touch my arm with that same hand. I was horrified, but being the good poker player, I am, he never saw or noticed my disgust. Then he picked his nose again. After that, I had to get up and leave the table because I couldn't take it anymore. I excused myself to use the restroom.

As I was getting ready to enter the restroom, Robert came up with an entire pitcher of tea. He looked at me and said, "Stop being so nice. If you don't leave, I will pour this whole pitcher of tea on you, and then you will have to leave." I told Robert I wouldn't need a tea bath because I already planned on telling Ray I was not feeling well and had to leave. Robert said, "If you even sit down at that table, this tea will be all over you." When I got back to the table and told Ray I was leaving, he asked if we could have dinner next time. I said, "I think we should keep our lives on a professional level."

Letting a restaurant help you isn't just for when you're going out with people you don't know. It can also be beneficial when you have a date with an acquaintance. Sometimes the staff, other customers, and you might be a little picky about the date's habits.

Darrel Had an Interesting Path to Finding His Love

Darrel met Angie in the local hardware store when she asked him if he knew which cordless drill worked the best. She explained she needed to do repairs on the wood fence in her yard. By the end of the shopping trip, they had exchanged numbers and agreed to meet for dinner and a movie the next Friday night. Darrel arrived at the restaurant first and was seated promptly. After about five minutes, Angie called to say she was running late and would be there in a couple of minutes. Thirty minutes later Darrel looked up to see Angie had finally arrived, but with another couple in tow. She explained she had run into her friends in the lobby, and they told her the wait for a table was now over forty-five minutes long. She then said to Darrel, "I hope it is okay; I invited them to join us for dinner." They all had a fabulous time. Erica and Stanley had a grand sense of humor, and everyone was laughing through the whole dinner. Darrel had purchased movie tickets online, and he wanted to get to the theater to get a good seat, so eventually he told the group it was time to wrap up dinner so they could get over to the theater. Everyone got very quiet, and then Erica said, "We all were hoping to go back to my place and play some games." Darrel told the group he didn't want to waste the tickets. Then Angie said, "These games are much more fun than going to any movie. We have more than a friendship; our games involve sex." Darrel, being a good Christian man, let them know he would be attending the movie alone.

When he got to the theater, he saw a woman in line who was obviously by herself. Darrel walked up to her and asked if she was a swinger. With a shocked look, she said, "No!" Darrel introduced himself, gave the woman his extra ticket and said, "Since we both are alone, we should sit together to watch the movie." And that was the start of a beautiful relationship. Lori and Darrel are now engaged to be married. These two good Christians give credit to swingers for helping them find their true love.

A Quick Stop to Pick up Some Money

I had a date one evening with Raj, a man from Kuwait who lives on the other side of my neighborhood. On our way to the restaurant, he asked if we could stop so he could pick up some cash. The next thing I knew, we were at a research center. Raj was part of a clinical research trial—in other words, he was a human guinea pig.

Apparently, in his mid-forties, he still received the money for all his living expenses from his father. Raj felt a job with hours to work was a little too constraining for his lifestyle, my first red flag, but I gave it a chance. He said, "If you join the research group, you could also get a little extra cash, and it would be a memorable first date." Thinking to myself that I could use a little extra cash, and this research wasn't too intrusive, I said, "Sure, why not." Anyone who knows me knows I am a good sport.

After we were done filling out the paperwork and giving them our blood, I said to Raj, "Why don't we just go back to my house, and I will cook us dinner?" Raj felt there were just too many people in my house for him to feel comfortable and asked if I could cook at his place, which was my second red flag. Against my better judgment and since I had been acquainted with him for a year, I agreed. On the way to his house, he picked up a case of beer and some hot dogs, chips, and buns, which was the third red flag. We finally got to his house, and he had to kick a pile of clothes out if the way for me to get into the kitchen. There were dirty dishes everywhere. I turned to look back at Raj; he was turning on the television and sitting down. Raj looked up at me, pointed around the room, and said, "You can start wherever you want." I burst out laughing and said, "What the heck are you talking about?" Raj answered that in his family, the women did all the cleaning, and I better get started.

I laughed and laughed as I walked out the door and down the street. It was so beneficial to have a cell phone and be able to call my friend to come to pick me up. Technology is grand!

Dating after Divorce

Phil Met Foxy on a Free Online Dating Site

Phil usually is a very "dot the I's, cross the t's" type of person. I don't know if it is because of his busy schedule or what, but for some reason, he didn't do his due diligence involving his online dating.

When Phil met Foxy on a free online dating site, like many others, she did not have a photo. A missing photo is always a huge red flag to me, and I did not hesitate to tell Phil just what I thought. People who do not have a picture are often trying to hide something, and that can be a problem. Phil didn't see it that way at all and said he could ask her to text him a photo. Well, she never did! Instead, she would send pictures of famous people with red hair and a caption saying, "I look like her, lol." After about a week of texting and talking on the phone, Phil asked Foxy to meet him at a sports bar near her home.

Foxy had told him to look for a foxy redhead with a blue shirt and jeans. As soon as he walked through the door, he saw a lovely and tall redhead. Phil walked up and said, "Hi, Foxy, you really are foxy." The very sexy lady replied in a British accent, "No, I am not, and you had better leave before my husband gets back from the loo." Phil apologized and politely excused himself.

On his way out the door, Phil met Foxy, who did have red hair. That was the only thing truthful about the description of herself. Phil didn't want to meet the other redhead's husband, so he suggested they go out to dinner. Foxy explained that they needed to go to her place first so she could change into a nicer outfit for dinner.

Upon their arrival at her apartment, a six-year-old came running up to Phil with a big smile and open arms, saying, "Are you, my new Daddy?" Phil explained he was just a friend but was wondering how many men this poor boy had asked that question. Foxy returned very quickly, hiding something behind her back. To Phil's surprise, she asked him, "Do you want to do a line of cocaine or smoke a joint before we go?" Phil very quickly explained he does not do drugs of any type, nor does he ever want to. He told Foxy he had gotten a text while she was changing and needed to get home. As Phil put it, that was the end of his "three-eighths date" with Foxy.

Blind Dates Can Be a Dream or a Nightmare

Have you ever had a friend set you up for a blind date with a "guy who would be perfect for you," only to experience the worst evening of your life? As a single woman in the city, I regularly had friends offering to set me up with some great guy they knew. I always waved away the suggestions until one day, my friend Leslie told me about her husband's college buddy, who had recently moved into the city. She said Jeffrey was tall, attractive, and educated, and raved about how perfect we would be together, so I let her pass along my number. I admit I was a little excited. I put some extra thought into what I would wear, touched up my roots, and headed out one evening to meet him at a favorite pub.

When Jeffrey arrived, I was pleasantly surprised. He was no gargoyle! He was attractive, well dressed, and smelled nice. So far, so good! We made a little small talk, ordered some food, started to relax, and then the nightmare began.

Our date became a kind of bizarre interview. I was ready to discuss the city and some favorite places, maybe a little personal information to pique his interest, but Jeffrey's questions started personal, became intrusive, and topped out at wildly inappropriate. He asked about my income, age, weight, eating habits, savings and investments, exercise, and on and on. After each question, he would expound upon how he liked "his women" to be. I learned that he wanted "his women" to be "under 115 pounds," "willing to put a lot of time into their bodies," "making really good money," "well off," "smart investors," "a few years younger" than him, and "really aware of what they put in their bodies," among other things.

The last straw? Jeffrey inquired about my "intimate activities." When I forced a laugh, saying that wasn't something I discussed an hour after meeting someone, he began telling me—in blush-inducing detail—what he liked "his women" to do! I had enough. I stood up, told him firmly that it was time for the date to end, and walked out.

The next day, I asked Leslie what she was thinking, and why she ever believed I might like Jeffrey. It turned out that she had never personally met him and had been going on her husband's glowing reviews. I question either the memory or the honesty of Leslie's husband!

If you want to avoid a similar nightmare, but still would like to enjoy the occasional blind date, take my advice: Make sure that the person suggesting they set up knows your potential date well. How long have they known them? How long has it been since they spent time together? What *exactly* makes them think you would hit it off? What are the person's current friends like? If they were single, would they date them? If your friend can't answer questions like these with positive information, be leery.

Since the nightmare with Jeffrey, I have followed my own advice. I've only had a few other bad experiences and met some wonderful men, one of whom I still take dance lessons when we both are available. If a friend wants to set you up with a "great person," keep these tips in mind, take a chance, and your blind date could be a dream instead of a nightmare—or a good dance partner and friend.

In the New Modern Blended Family: Even If You Had Nothing to Do with It ...

Lindsey and John have a modern blended family. They both had gotten along very well with John's ex-wife until the weekend they were planning to go on vacation with all the kids. It was just an overnight camping trip about an hour from home. When you have six kids, and two are in diapers, you don't travel far. They picked up John's kids early because they wanted to set up camp before dark and also needed to run home to get a few things, like a diaper bag and wipes. Finally, they were on their way but needed to stop at a store for supplies. Lindsey had the responsibility of taking the kids for a potty break and diaper changes before they hit the road. John was tasked with picking up a few things and grabbing an extra tent. Upon exiting the restroom, all three of John and his ex's children went running up to his ex, who was in the store, yelling, "Mommy!" The man who she was with turned to her and said, "Mommy? I didn't know you had children". Then he kept looking at John's oldest son, saying, "Really, how old are you? And is she your mom?" After that, he looked at her and said, "We need to go and talk right now!"

We have determined that she must be in a midlife crisis or something. It turned out he was her new boyfriend, and he was told she didn't have children! The new beau was about fifteen years younger than her, and she had also lied about her age. Somehow this woman had decided it was all Lindsey's fault that she lost this wonderful man.

As you can see, dating after divorce can be full of surprises, some pleasant, and some not so pleasant. Mistakes and setbacks are part of the process, but rest assured that whatever you're going through, you're not alone, and maybe your lousy date will become a funny story shared with friends in years to come.

Dating after Divorce

The Heart Knows

The heart knows

How many beats per minute it goes

Every heart knows.

Quietly a wind blows—and then there are crescendos;

Undeniably a wind knows

Every mile per hour it goes.

So in an hour, a minute, or a secondary guess,

Tell me how do we know much less …

   … Than our hearts confess my friend?

      Can it be because our best
      Is blowing in the wind?
      And we don't have the heart
      To rest and simply breathe it in.

—Tony Haynes

Dating after Divorce

Little Bitty Babies

*T*he little bitty babies
*H*ave a way of charming
*E*veryone.

*G*od puts a bit more of Himself in
*O*ur daughters & sons,
*O*ften delighting us with
*D*elicate doses of goodness spun—God spins
   but we spawn ...

*I*nnocence dormant in our
*N*ature thus far

*L*ittle bitty babies remind us of who we are.
*I*ntegral parts
*F*rom a flawless façade
*E*ach in first person ...
... *A child of God.*

                                    —***Tony Haynes***

Chapter 11

Patience, Caution, and a Sense of Humor

Take dating after divorce at your own pace; it's meant to be fun and refreshing. You are a vibrant, beautiful person with a great deal to offer potential friends and dating partners. Keep these essential points in mind as you meet new people and search for love:

- Wait until you're ready! There's no need to rush into dating. Take the time to date yourself first.
- Trust yourself and the people who know you best.
- Think of every date as an opportunity to make a new friend.
- Consider online dating but be sure to craft your own profile and screen potential dates thoroughly.

- Be careful! Conducting background checks, meeting in a public place, and arranging safety measures ahead of dates are all great ways to keep yourself safe.
- Take a break from dating if you need to; dating should be fun, not a chore.
- Be a perspicacious dater. You are a person of value, and you deserve to find the partner who's right for you. While you're looking for the right person, you're also finding out more about yourself, and that's a great thing!

With patience, caution, and a sense of humor, you'll find that dating after divorce is a grand adventure, one that will truly help you turn lemons into zesty lemon sorbet! You may be divorced, but you are now *Divorced and Scared NO More*!!!

Dating after Divorce

Connectivity

I connected with you on a plain so high
The connection grew as rain passed by.
Affection knew from a first night kiss
To sustained last sigh, it would be like this.

You connected with me—As you are, forthright;
Connectivity made the stars highlight
Our proclivity, to deflect sun spots
And with mars in sight, we connected dots.

As two, who retain lost time
Re-connecting through all paradigms,
We've elected to be a most eclectic brew
You connected with me—and me connected with you.

—**Tony Haynes**

Zesty Lemon Sorbet

Ingredients

- 1/2 cup honey
- 3/4 cup carbonated mineral water
- 3/4 cup fresh lemon juice
- 1 teaspoon lemon zest
- 4 shots low-calorie lemon-flavored vodka
- Drizzle lemon liqueur to taste

Directions

1. Mix honey, water, lemon juice, zest, and vodka.
2. Pour the mixture into a shallow container and place in the freezer, fluffing with a fork occasionally until it is semi-frozen. Return to the freezer until frozen solid.
3. After it has frozen, remove it from the freezer and let sit for 5 minutes.
4. Run it through a food processor or blender until smooth.
5. Place sorbet in an airtight container and freeze until ready to serve.
6. Serve as you would ice cream and drizzle with lemon liqueur.

Dating after Divorce

Through the Toughest Times

*T*ough times
*H*ave a way of disappearing from view,
*A*nd cloudy days have a way of clearing up, too.
*N*othing is as it was—due to the
*K*indness that you've shown me.

*Y*ou know me like no
*O*ne else has known me,
*U*nderstand my needs before your doorbell chimes …

… *And that's what gets me through the toughest times.*

—Tony Haynes

Dating after Divorce

I Am My Own Hero

I am my own hero;
I rescue me
From dragons & dungeons.
I bungee jump,
I take the plunge in
A life I attest to
Never less than zero.

> *I am my own hero & personal savior*
> *On my best behavior,*
> *A role model*
> *At the helm & throttle.*
> *Aristotle*
> *Running with wisdom up the middle,*
> *I don't fiddle with Nero.*

I am my own hero,
I am not a sandwich
Or the type of man, which
His plans switch
On a whim
When life's a bitch.
The God in me, I honor Him
When it's sink or swim.
This is how it has to be
I make my own way,
I save my own day,
I am a hero to me.

—Tony Haynes

About the Authors

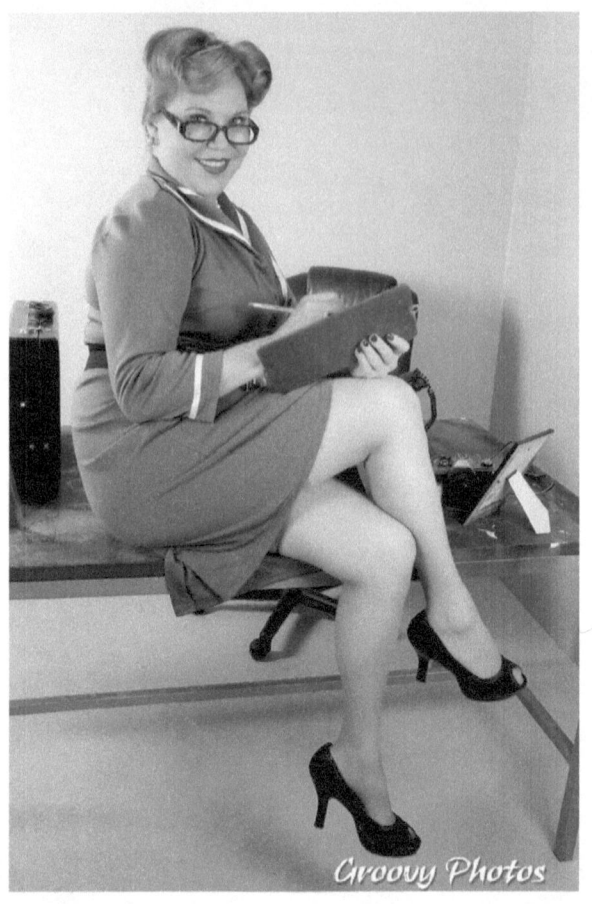

Tasher aka Tammy Asher divorced on her 26th wedding anniversary, and she embarked on a new life. Her marriage was broken all to pieces; she was not going to let the divorce break her. Tasher quickly discovered that single life was very different from all those years ago. One case in point is dating; there was not an internet back then, and cell phones didn't exist. Like many, she initially was scared but being a smart businessperson; she set up a plan of how to date yet continue to keep her and family safe.

Tasher has dyslexia yet always enjoyed writing and decided to share with others the things she learned while rebuilding her life. The launch of Divorced and Scared No More was November 2012 and quickly received a worldwide following. As she started sharing her experiences, others in-turn shared some of their stories. The intent of the site was for people to share without fear of reprisals. The logo for the website inspiration was a set of broken pilot wings (her ex-husband is a pilot). The website has since closed down, but there is a Facebook page still available.

Tasher is not a professional therapist; rather, she is sharing because she has "been there and done that" and understands how it FEELS. No two people will have identical situations. She hopes that the shared experiences will guide others through this time in their life with the least amount of trepidation.

Tammys' quest to help others forgive the past and rejoice in their new life did not stop with the website or DASNM book series. She has contributed to

DivorceSupportCenter.com, HopeAfterDivorce.org, The Good Men Project, Single Sassy Mom (dot) com. She has had guest appearances on John Brislin Show, David Essel Alive! and Developing a New YOU. Guest Co-Host on Single Again Now What and The Divorce View. The Ed Tyll show did an entire show highlighting Tasher and DASNM.com. She is also involved with the

Tough Angels Organizations; The Wedding Rings Project and Wings of Hope. Plus, the Acts of Random Kindness and ARK Harbor

Tasher is single and a mother of three adult children and a proud Grammy to three grandchildren. She lives in Houston, TX with her daughter, two grandchildren, two dogs, three cats, and the occasional rescue animal. You can follow Tasher on FB Divorced and Scared NO More and Twitter @Divorced_Scared. You can watch her on YouTube, "What is Forgiveness." "The Internet, Your Ex, and the Legal System" and "How Do I Know When I am Ready to Date."

Tony Haynes is a lyricist/songwriter/author/philosopher and a practitioner of Acrostic Poetry. In less than a minute Tony can literally pull words out of thin air. Give him the title of what you'd like to call your poem, or song and he will create it for you on the spot. The catch is, he will write your name in the air, and show you how the beginning of each line in the work he's creating spells the letters of your name downward. It's an eloquent combination of spontaneous penmanship & showmanship. He calls it "Creativity in an Instant."

Before Tony realized he had this rare poetic talent, he was and still is a prolific lyricist, songwriter, music publisher and record producer. In this capacity, Tony has accomplished a great deal. "Send A Little Love," his first song, was recorded by the Spinners in 1981. Since then, Tony's songs have been recorded on over 200 albums, selling in excess of 60 million copies worldwide. These songs have earned him 60 gold and multi-platinum awards, as well as several ASCAP Awards. He has collaborated with the most successful writers and producers in the world. Rather than leave anyone out, feel free see Tony's **Wikipedia** page for more detail on this aspect of his creative life.

In 1993, Tony turned his considerable talents to the world of children's entertainment. He began producing audio products, writing books and creating animated characters. Tony has authored 34 children's books based on the Baby Looney Tunes characters. Tony has also the author of several books' adults will enjoy such as *Reincarnation of Douglas Kavanaugh.*

Tony has added 'spoken word artist' to the hats he seems to juggle seamlessly. A collaboration with French composer, Stephane d'Esposito. *The Pianist and The Poet* is elegant and romantic production

Last but certainly not least, Tony is also executive producing and creating original programming for television. He has several shows in development based on his novels and scripts.

Contact and Links

Tasher aka Tammy Asher

Email hbty18@gmail.com

Facebook DivorcedAndScaredNoMore

Twitter @Divorced_Scared

YouTube T asher

Tony Haynes

P.O. Box 201

Lancaster, CA 93584

http://www.tonyhaynes.webs.com

https://en.wikipedia.org/wiki/Tony_Haynes

https://www.reverbnation.com/tonyhaynes

Justin Nutt, LSCSW, LAC

Lead therapist at Anderson County Mental Health, Clinical Editor, and Board Member at Social Justice Solutions. Author of The Good Guy, the Bad Guy, and The Ugly Truth, Stories of Survivors: Stories from those who have overcome abuse.

Tracey West

http://www.traceywest.co.uk

Sandraspeed Formatting Expert

Email sandraspeed@writeme.com

Lamont Johnson Jr – Groovy Photos

http://www.modelmayhem.com/692015

https://www.facebook.com/GroovyPhotos/?pnref=about.overview

Dating after Divorce

***

Dear Reader,

Thank you, so much for buying Dating after Divorce—From Lemons to Zesty Lemon Sorbet. It is the third book in the Divorced and Scared NO More three-book series. I want to thank you for being one of our readers!

I hope that you've enjoyed reading the book. I want to make sure this book provided you with the value you needed.

If you have ANY issues or feedback, please email me at HBTY18@gmail.com. The only way I can improve the books are with your help. I would be honored to get your honest opinion of this book in the review section where you purchased the book!

Thank you again for reading my book. I truly appreciate your business and hope it the book helped you during this time of your transformation. If you haven't yet, please play either version of the song with two names, "Faith of the Heart" also known as "Where My Heart Will Take Me." Diane Warren wrote the first version and performed by Rod Stewart for the soundtrack to the 1998 film Patch Adams. English tenor Russell Watson also recorded it as "Where My Heart Will Take Me" to be used as a theme to the 2001 television series Star Trek: Enterprise. Now it is the time for you to soar and reach for the stars! ***Now it is time for you to soar and reach for the stars!***

Wishing you the best,

Tammy Asher aka Tasher

P.S If you no longer find a need for this book, pleases pass it on to someone who can benefit from it.

www.ingramcontent.com/pod-product-compliance
Lightning Source LLC
Chambersburg PA
CBHW031617210526
45464CB00004B/1615